THE ARCHITECTURE OF HUMANISM

1. *The Architecture of Humanism*. Interior court of the Palazzo Farnese, Rome.

THE ARCHITECTURE

OF

HUMANISM

A Study in the History of Taste

By Geoffrey Scott

With a portfolio of photographs

The Norton Library
W·W·NORTON & COMPANY·INC·
NEW YORK

To Cecil Pinsent

PHOTOGRAPHIC CREDITS

John Barrington Bayley, 1, 5, 6, 16, 20, 21, 23, 25, 27; H. Stafford Bryant, Jr., 2, 3, 7–10, 13, 14, 19; Alison Frantz, 4; Lafayette College, 11; New York Public Library, 22; Henry Hope Reed, 17, 18, 24, 26; Southern Methodist University, 15.

First published in the Norton Library 1974
by arrangement with Constable & Company Limited

Books That Live
The Norton imprint on a book means that in the publisher's
estimation it is a book not for a single season but for the years.
W. W. Norton & Company, Inc.

Library of Congress Cataloging in Publication Data
Scott, Geoffrey, 1885–1929.
  The architecture of humanism.
  (The Norton library)
  Includes bibliographical references.
  1. Architecture. 2. Aesthetics. I. Title.
NA2500.S4 1974   724   74-14765
ISBN 0-393-00734-0

Printed in the United States of America
3 4 5 6 7 8 9 0

When *The Architecture of Humanism* by Geoffrey Scott appeared in 1914, it was hailed by some as the finest book on architecture since the days of John Ruskin. Others, less generous, at least conceded that it was certainly to be admired for the beauty of its prose. Whatever the reception and subsequent opinion, it remains among the outstanding works of this century on the subject of architecture.

The book's fascination stems largely from the fact that Geoffrey Scott offers the clearest analysis of the theories and ideas behind much of 19th- and 20th-century architecture—theories and ideas universally held today. But the reader must not let the brilliant analysis obscure what is really the heart of the book: a discussion of the classical tradition as reflected in the architecture of Renaissance and Baroque Italy and the role given the human body in contributing to that tradition.

Geoffrey Scott was well fitted for the ambitious job he set himself. He was born on June 11, 1884, at Hampstead, London, the son of a prosperous flooring manufacturer. He obtained a standard classical education at Rugby School and, in 1903, he entered New College, Oxford. There he won the Newdigate Poetry Prize and the Chancellor's English Essay Prize, the latter for an essay entitled "The National Character of English Architecture."

Quite obviously architecture was an early interest. He could easily have gone into journalism, because C. P. Scott, editor of *The Manchester Guardian*, was his uncle. Instead, however, he went off to Italy in 1907, joining the landscape architect, Cecil Pinsent, in Florence. That same year he became librarian and secretary to the art expert and historian, Bernard Berenson. "B.B." had only just negotiated a contract with Joseph Duveen by the terms of which, for the handsome retainer of £20,000 a year, he would pass on the authenticity of pictures and other objects of art submitted for evaluation by the dealer. With the money Berenson bought the villa, *I Tatti*, in nearby Fiesole (it is now owned by Harvard University) and there he and his wife, Mary, received and entertained on a most generous scale. Scott became part of the household.

The pre-1914 world of Anglo-American Florence was not all parties, cards, gossip and sightseeing; energy and money were often spent in renovating and building villas and gardens. It was there that Diego Suarez, America's greatest living landscape architect, did his first gardens, revealing the genius that was to produce the magnificent gardens of Villa Vizcaya (the Dade County Art Museum) in Miami. Geoffrey Scott himself was to practice architecture modestly in association with Cecil Pinsent. Together they designed the library and gardens of *I Tatti* and the neighboring villa and gardens of *Le Balze* for Professor Charles A. Strong, George Santayana's close friend who had married the oldest daughter of John D. Rockefeller.

"Though I lived in partnership with him for four or five years," Pinsent recalled of Scott, "ours was a partnership of opposites, complementary gifts, each one having what the other did not have . . ." It was while sharing quarters with Pinsent that Scott wrote *The Architecture of Humanism*. Yet it was not with his partner, to whom he gave the dedication, that he talked of the book but with Mary Berenson, "and with her at *I Tatti*," Pinsent wrote, "he used to sit up till all hours of the night discussing it." Mary Berenson, the sister of the essayist Logan Pearsall Smith, had encouraged her husband in his writings and now she provided incentive for Scott.

With the riches of Italy at his door he absorbed the classical tradition in all its forms, ancient and modern. He knew, as so many have since forgotten, that it represents the main stream of Western art. From the vantage of the Italian scene Scott became aware that the stream had been muddied by such men as the Gothic Revivalist A. W. N. Pugin, the exhorter John Ruskin, the French restorer and theorist Eugène-Emanuel Viollet-le-Duc, William Morris, and others. Their ideas were derived from sources outside of art—namely from poetry, science, morals, and philosophy. These ideas, from which the dominant concepts of contemporary art are derived, Scott put into perspective by the device of calling them "fallacies."

Typical of the concepts is Louis Sullivan's well known "form follows function." It means that a building's use and its type of construction must dictate the outward appearance. Although still a popular axiom, it is not accepted with quite the degree of reverence it was a generation ago. Scott saw such a concept and its variations as originating in science and engineering, and, therefore, he set it in the category of "The Mechanical Fallacy." Part of the same "Fallacy" would be the contemporary notion that only by adopting new materials and new methods of construction can a new style of architecture be attained. The widespread use of marble, travertine, and limestone facing in modern design shows that the idea, while current in theory, is often disregarded in practice.

The very notion of the self-conscious pursuit of a new, a unique style—aside from questions of method in attaining it—has its sources in literature. It is part of the notion of originality, more especially originality for its own sake, seen in the cult of self-expression. As a concept it matured in Romantic literature, and for that reason Scott listed it as part of "The Romantic Fallacy."

The term, *fallacy*, has an element of shock because it

throws into question ideas which we have come—perhaps too casually—to accept without reflection. This can be seen when "The Romantic Fallacy" is extended to make the architect society's prime mover and shaker. In recent times no one has stated this aspect of the profession more definitely than the late Le Corbusier, a disciple of Viollet-le-Duc: "It is a question of building which is at the root of social unrest today: architecture or revolution." Then there is also the strong anti-urban outlook of such American architects and city planners as Frank Lloyd Wright, whose acceptance of a simplistic interpretation of nature as a philosophical mainspring for urban design is very romantic.

If one were to identify the common denominator of contemporary architecture it would probably be the absence of ornament. It is even so in the United States where one of the heroes of present-day American architecture is Louis Sullivan, recognized in his own time as the country's most fertile ornamentalist. Contemporary theory regards ornament as "false" since it conceals the "true" nature of construction and materials. For Scott, however, this theory was a misapplication of a moral concept to things physical, and he called it part of "The Ethical Fallacy."

To the last of his four fallacies Scott gave the name "Biological." For him it meant the application of 19th-century theories of scientific evolution to the history of architecture—and to all of art history, for that matter. The evolutionary approach seeks to explain styles, buildings, and objects of art by examining antecedents. It is shown in the frequent use of the words, "influence" and "problem" in art history, the "influence" being the antecedents and the "problem" their identification. Buildings and art objects are regarded as parts of an historical sequence, and thus little emphasis is given to arriving at value judgments or to analysing why an object of art is beautiful.

If Scott has put us on the defensive with his fallacies—

and for some he may appear harsh as well as mistaken—
we instinctively come back with a query: if so much of
the theory that governed the architecture of the last
century and that still governs architecture today is fallacious, we ask, what is the alternative? Scott anticipates
us on this score by asking us to consider the classical
tradition.

We today are not quite so disdainful of the classical
as were the more outspoken architectural critics of the
last century and of a generation ago. Even the "American
Renaissance" that began in the 1880's and disappeared
around 1930—the last full flourish of the Renaissance
that had begun in Italy in the 15th century—is being
shown a new respect. Evidence enough for that is found
in the growing battle for the nation's great landmarks,
the outstanding example being the abortive attempt to
save Pennsylvania Station in New York City several
years ago. So when Scott proposes that Renaissance and
Baroque architecture had its source in an academic tradition we are curious rather than mocking. The academic
tradition, in his thesis, consists of a "canon of forms"—
that is to say, a standard fixed by the great buildings,
monuments, and sculpture of Imperial Rome. There is
no theory to study. Instead, study means examining,
drawing, and even measuring ancient works. The method
produced the classical wonders of Italy; it also produced
our National Capitol and the chief ornaments of the
American Renaissance.

Our inclination is to dismiss Scott's alternative because the academic tradition is simply not part of art
today. But Scott went further and dwelt on the importance of an awareness of the human body's role in
art. This awareness goes beyond the use of the human
form in painting and sculpture and consists in our unconsciously transcribing our physical selves into terms
of architecture and architecture into terms of our physical
selves. This is what he understood to be humanism. For
him the virtue of the Italian Renaissance and Baroque

was the importance given the visual response of the beholder. The direct physical reaction to what we see Scott called taste, "the disinterested enthusiasm for architectural form."

Admittedly, the human figure, when it appears in contemporary art, does so in fragments and distortions, and it sometimes seems that humanism has been wholly rejected by today's architects. Yet Scott, going beyond the immediate presence of the human body, pursues the role of our physical response to more abstract humanist values, those of mass, space, and line. He dwells particularly on the sense of space, a part of his humanism that has a very familiar ring. Scott anticipated much of the current discussion among architects of this key element. It is true that what he had in mind was space replete with ornament, or he would not have based his argument on the Renaissance and the Baroque. No matter the style, space is a monopoly of all architecture, he pointed out, and for that reason must be considered a primary factor.

Nothing is more volatile in our time than artistic fashion. What appears to be so successful at the moment is forgotten tomorrow. The growing enthusiasm for the preservation of landmarks bespeaks a restlessness with current architecture on the part of both the public and the profession. For those who are seeking an answer, Geoffrey Scott offers a most attractive one, the architecture of humanism.

Scott's subsequent career had little to do with architecture. The outbreak of the Great War at the time of the book's publication forced him into other paths. He remained in Italy, attached to the British Embassy in Rome. In 1918 he married the widow of William Bayard Cutting of New York, and his connections with I Tatti came to an end. In 1920 he was again at the British Embassy, as Press Secretary.

He talked of a sequel to The Architecture of Humanism, and of a book on Bernini (Bernini's Piazza San Pietro was his favorite work of architecture in Rome. Other

favorites were the interiors of the Gésu and San Ignazio)
but they were not to be. A small volume of verse, *A Box
of Paints*, did appear in 1923 and two years later he saw
published *A Portrait of Zélide*, the story of Madame de
Charrière, a lady who had enchanted the young James
Boswell. His friend, Edith Wharton, read the book in
manuscript and was warm in her praise, as were many
others. By now settled in England, he started on a biography of Boswell when he was approached in 1927 by
Colonel Ralph H. Isham to edit the famous Boswell papers, now in the Sterling Library of Yale University. Scott
accepted the invitation and worked on the papers, editing
the first six volumes. In the summer of 1929 he was in this
country when he came down with pneumonia. He was
taken to the Rockefeller Institute in New York City, and
there he died on August 14th at the age of forty-five.

In another age Geoffrey Scott would be held in high
honor. As it is, he is not to be found in the *Dictionary of
National Biography*, the English equivalent of the *Dictionary of American Biography*, and *The Architecture of
Humanism* is out of print in England.

It may well be asked: Why is it possible to have an
American edition? The answer is to be found in the fact
that the classical tradition persists vigorously in America
—in new churches, in new suburban houses, in new buildings on a number of university campuses, in much res-
toration work of recent years, and especially in interior
decoration. It may be an important sign that a society
called Classical America has been founded to promote
the classical in American art. The society assumes that it
is now time to plan a future which will be largely classical in the visual arts, for the classical tradition will continue to be the main artistic current of Western culture.
For Americans who take this point of view, *The Architecture of Humanism* is an esssential text.

The portfolio of illustrations, many of them never before published, has been prepared for the Norton Library
edition by H. Stafford Bryant, Jr.

HENRY HOPE REED, *New York City*

2. *The American Renaissance*. Dome of the Pasadena City Hall, by Arthur Brown, Jr.

The scope of this book requires a word of explanation, since from a very simple purpose it has developed to a rather complicated issue. My intention had been to formulate the chief principles of classical design in architecture. I soon realised that in the present state of our thought no theory of art could be made convincing, or even clear, to any one not already persuaded of its truth. There may, at the present time, be a lack of architectural taste: there is, unfortunately, no lack of architectural opinion. Architecture, it is said, must be 'expressive of its purpose' or 'expressive of its true construction' or 'expressive of the materials it employs' or 'expressive of the national life' (whether noble or otherwise) or 'expressive of a noble life' (whether national or not); or expressive of the craftsman's temperament, or the owner's or the architect's, or, on the contrary, 'academic' and studiously indifferent to these factors. It must, we are told, be symmetrical, or it must be picturesque—that is, above all things, unsymmetrical. It must be 'traditional' and 'scholarly,' that is, resembling what has already been done by Greek, Roman, Mediæval or Georgian architects, or it must be 'original' and 'spontaneous,' that is, it must be at pains to avoid this resemblance; or it must strike some happy compromise between these opposites; and so forth indefinitely.

If these axioms were frankly untrue, they would be easy to dismiss; if they were based on fully reasoned theories, they would be easy, at any rate, to discuss. They are neither. We have few 'fully reasoned' theories, and these, it will be seen, are flagrantly at variance with the facts to be explained. We subsist on a number of architectural habits, on scraps of tradition, on caprices and prejudices, and above all on this mass of more or less specious axioms, of

8

half-truths, unrelated, uncriticised and often contradictory, by means of which there is no building so bad that it cannot with a little ingenuity be justified, or so good that it cannot plausibly be condemned.

Under these circumstances, discussion is almost impossible, and it is natural that criticism should become dogmatic. Yet dogmatic criticism is barren, and the history of architecture, robbed of any standard of value, is barren also.

It appears to me that if we desire any clearness in this matter, we are driven from a priori æsthetics to the history of taste, and from the history of taste to the history of ideas. It is, I believe, from a failure to appreciate the true relation of taste to ideas, and the influence which each has exerted on the other, that our present confusion has resulted.

I have attempted, consequently, in the very narrow field with which this book is concerned, to trace the natural history of our opinions, to discover how far upon their own premisses they are true or false, and to explain why, when false, they have yet remained plausible, powerful, and, to many minds, convincing.

This is to travel far from the original question. Yet I believe the inquiry to be essential, and I have sought to keep it within the rigorous limit of a single argument. On these points the reader will decide.

So far as this study is concerned with the culture of the Italian Renaissance, I am indebted, as every student must always be indebted, primarily to Burckhardt. I have profited also by Wölfflin's Renaissance und Barock. To the friendship of Mr. Bernhard Berenson I owe a stimulus and encouragement which those who share it will alone appreciate. Mr. Francis Jekyll of the British Museum has kindly corrected my proofs.

5 VIA DELLE TERME,
FLORENCE,
February 14, 1914.

An epilogue at the end of the volume contains what I have wished to add in this edition.

There are a few changes in the text; but these do not affect the argument of the book.

G. S.

March 1924.

3. *The Rococo as Humanistic Design*. Detail of the interior of the abbey church at St. Gallen, Switzerland.

CONTENTS

Illustrations between pages 96 and 97

The Architecture of Humanism

'Well-building hath three conditions: Commodity, Firmness, and Delight.' From this phrase of an English humanist[1] a theory of architecture might take its start. Architecture is a focus where three separate purposes have converged. They are blended in a single method; they are fulfilled in a single result; yet in their own nature they are distinguished from each other by a deep and permanent disparity. The criticism of architecture has been confused in its process; it has built up strangely diverse theories of the art, and the verdicts it has pronounced have been contradictory in the extreme. Of the causes which have contributed to its failure, this is the chief: that it has sought to force on architecture an unreal unity of aim. 'Commodity, firmness, and delight'; between these three values the criticism of architecture has insecurely wavered, not always distinguishing very clearly between them, seldom attempting any statement of the relation they bear to one another, never pursuing to their conclusion the consequences which they involve. It has leaned now this way and now that, and struck, between these incommensurable virtues, at different points, its arbitrary balance.

Architecture, the most complex of the arts, offers to its critics many paths of approach, and as many opportunities for avoiding their goal. At the outset of a fresh study in this field, it is well, at the risk of pedantry, to define where these paths lead.

Architecture requires 'firmness.' By this necessity it

---

[1] Sir Henry Wotton, *Elements of Architecture*. He is adapting Vitruvius, Bk. i. chap. iii.

stands related to science, and to the standards of science. The mechanical bondage of construction has closely circumscribed its growth. Thrust and balance, pressure and its support, are at the root of the language which architecture employs. The inherent characters of marble, brick, wood and iron have moulded its forms, set limits to its achievement, and governed, in a measure, even its decorative detail. On every hand the study of architecture encounters physics, statics, and dynamics, suggesting, controlling, justifying its design. It is open to us, therefore, to look in buildings for the logical expression of material properties and material laws. Without these, architecture is impossible, its history unintelligible. And if, finding these everywhere paramount, we seek, in terms of material properties and material laws, not merely to account for the history of architecture, but to assess its value, then architecture will be judged by the exactness and sincerity with which it expresses constructive facts, and conforms to constructive laws. That will be the scientific standard for architecture: a logical standard so far as architecture is related to science, and no further.

But architecture requires 'commodity.' It is not enough that it should possess its own internal coherence, its abstract logic of construction. It has come into existence to satisfy an external need. That, also, is a fact of its history. Architecture is subservient to the general uses of mankind. And, immediately, politics and society, religion and liturgy, the large movements of races and their common occupations, become factors in the study. These determine what shall be built, and, up to a point, in what way. The history of civilisation thus leaves in architecture its truest, because its most unconscious record. If, then, it is legitimate to consider architecture as an expression of mechanical laws, it is legitimate, no less, to see in it an expression of human life. This furnishes a standard of value totally distinct from the scientific. Buildings may be judged by the success with which they supply the practical ends they are designed to meet. Or, by a natural extension, we may judge them by the value of those ends themselves; that is to say, by the external purposes which they reflect. These, indeed, are two very different questions. The last makes a moral reference which the first avoids, but both spring, and spring inevitably, from the link which architecture has with life—from that 'condition of well-building' which Wotton calls commodity.

And architecture requires 'delight.' For this reason, interwoven with practical ends and their mechanical solutions, we may trace in architecture a third and different factor—the disinterested desire for beauty. This desire does not, it is true, culminate here in a purely æsthetic *result*, for it has to deal with a concrete basis which is ultilitarian. It is, none the less, a purely æsthetic *impulse*, an impulse distinct from all the others which architecture may simultaneously satisfy, an impulse by virtue of which architecture becomes art. It is a separate instinct. Sometimes it will borrow a suggestion from the laws of firmness or commodity; sometimes it will run counter to them, or be offended by the forms they would dictate. It has its own standard, and claims its own authority. It is possible, therefore, to ask how far, and how successfully, in any architectural style, this æsthetic impulse has been embodied; how far, that is to say, the instincts which, in the other arts, exert an obvious and unhampered activity, have succeeded in realising themselves also through this more complicated and more restricted instrument. And we can ask, still further, whether there may not be æsthetic instincts, for which this instrument, restricted as it is, may furnish the sole and peculiar expression. This is to study architecture, in the strict sense, as an art.

Here, then, are three 'conditions of well-building,' and corresponding to them three modes of criticism, and three provinces of thought.

Now what, in fact, is the result? The material data of our study we certainly possess in abundance: the statistics of architecture, the history of existing works, their shape and size and authorship, have long been investigated with the highest scholarship. But when we ask to be given not history but criticism, when we seek to know what is the value of these works of art, viewed in themselves or by comparison with one another, and why they are to be considered worthy of this exact attention, and whether one is to be considered more deserving of it than another, and on what grounds, the answers we obtain may be ready and numerous, but they are certainly neither consistent nor clear.

The criticism of architecture has been of two kinds. The first of these remains essentially historical. It is content to describe the conditions under which the styles of the past arose. It accepts the confused and partly fortuitous phenomenon which architecture actually is, and estimates the phenomenon by a method as confused and fortuitous as itself. It passes in and out of the three provinces of thought, and relates its subject now to science, now to art, and now to life. It treats of these upon a single plane, judging one building by standards of constructive skill, another by standards of rhythm and proportion, and a third by standards of practical use or by the moral impulse of its builders. This medley of elements, diverse and uncommensurated as they are, can furnish no general estimate or true comparison of style.

Doubtless, *as a matter of history*, architecture has not come into existence in obedience to any *a priori* æsthetic. It has grown up around the practical needs of the race, and in satisfying these it has been deflected, now by the obstinate claims of mechanical laws, now by a wayward search for beauty. But the problem of the architect and that of the critic are here essentially different. The work of the architect is synthetic. He must take into simultaneous account our three 'conditions of well-building,' and find some compromise which keeps a decent peace between their claims. The task of the critic, on the contrary, is one of analysis. He has to discover, define, and maintain the ideal standards of value in each province. Thus the three standards of architecture, united in practice, are separable, and must be separated, in thought. Criticism of the historical type fails to apply an ideal and consistent anal ysis, for the insufficient reason that the *practice* of architecture has, of necessity, been neither consistent nor ideal. Such criticism is not necessarily misleading. Its fault is more often that it leads nowhere. Its judgments may be individually accurate, but it affords us no general view, for it adopts no fixed position. It is neither simple, nor comprehensive, nor consistent. It cannot, therefore, furnish a theory of style.

The second type of criticism is more dangerous. For the sake of simplicity it lays down some 'law' of architectural taste. Good design in architecture, it will say, should 'express the uses the building is intended to serve'; 'it should faithfully state the facts of its construction,' or again it should 'reflect the life of a noble civilisation.' Then, having made these plausible assumptions, it drives its theory to a conclusion, dwells on the examples that support its case, and is willing, for the sake of consistency, to condemn all architecture in which the theory is not confirmed. Such general anathemas are flattering alike to the author and his reader. They greatly simplify the subject. They have a show of logic. But they fail to explain why the styles of architecture which they find it necessary to condemn have in fact been created and admired. Fashion consequently betrays these faultless arguments; for whatever has once genuinely pleased is likely to be again found pleasing; art and the enjoyment of art continue in the condemned paths undismayed; and criticism is left to discover a sanction for them, if it can, in some new theory, as simple, as logical, and as insufficient as the first.

The true task of criticism is to understand such æsthetic pleasures as have in fact been felt, and then to draw whatever laws and conclusions it may from that understanding. But no amount of reasoning will create, or can annul, an æsthetic experience; for the aim of the arts has not been logic, but delight. The theory of architecture, then, requires logic; but it requires, not less, an independent sense of beauty. Nature, unfortunately, would seem to unite these qualities with extreme reluctance.

Obviously, there is room for confusion. The 'condition of delight' in architecture—its value as an art—may conceivably be found to consist in its firmness, or in its commodity, or in both; or it may consist in something else different from, yet dependent upon these; or it may be independent of them altogether. In any case, these elements are, at first sight, distinct. There is no reason, *prima facie*, to suppose that there exists between them a pre-established harmony, and that in consequence a perfect principle of building can be laid down which should, in full measure, satisfy them all. And, in the absence of such a principle, it is quite arbitrary to pronounce dogmatically on the concessions which art should make to science or utility. Unless it can be proved that these apparently different values are in reality commensurable, there ought to be three separate schemes of criticism: the first based on construction, the second on convenience, the third on æsthetics. Each could be rational, complete, and, within its own province, valid. Thus by degrees might be obtained what at present is certainly lacking—the data for a theory of architecture which should not be contradicted at once by the history of taste.

The present study seeks to explain one chapter of that history. It deals with a limited period of architecture, from a single point of view.

The period is one which presents a certain obvious unity. It extends from the revival of classical forms at the hands of Brunelleschi, in the fifteenth century, to the rise of the Gothic movement, by which, four hundred years later, they were eclipsed. The old mediævalism, and the new, mark the boundaries of our subject. At no point in the four centuries which intervened does any line of cleavage occur as distinct as those which sever the history of architecture at these two points. And between them there is no true halting-place. Thus the term 'Renaissance architecture,' which originally denoted no more than the earlier stages, has gradually and inevitably come to be extended to the work of all this period.

It is true that during these years many phases of architectural style, opposed in aim and contradictory in feeling, successively arose; but the language in which they disputed was one language, the dialects they employed were all akin; and at no moment can we say that what follows is not linked to what went before by common reference to a great tradition, by a general participation in a single complex of ideas. And incompatible as these several phases— the primitive, classic, baroque, academic, rococo—may at their climax appear to be, yet, for the most part, they grew from one another by gradual transitions. The margins which divide them are curiously difficult to define. They form, in fact, a complete chapter in architecture, to be read consecutively and as a whole. But at the two moments with which our study begins and ends, the sequence of architecture is radically cleft. The building of the Pazzi Chapel in Florence marks a clear break with the mediæval past, and with it rises a tradition which was never fundamentally deserted, until in the nineteenth century traditionalism itself was cast aside.

It is in Italy, where Renaissance architecture was native, that we shall follow this tradition. The architecture of France in the seventeenth and eighteenth centuries and, in a lesser degree, that of the Georgian period in England, might furnish brilliant examples of the same manner of building. The Italian experiment enabled the architects of France, amid their more favourable environment, to create a succession of styles, in some ways more splendid, and certainly more exquisite and complete. Yet, if we wish to watch architectural energy where it is most concentrated, most vigorous, and most original it is to Italy that we must turn. And in a study which is to deal rather with the principles than with the history of Renaissance architecture, it will be convenient thus to restrict its scope.

From what point of view should this architecture be

judged so as best to reveal its unity and its intent? A general survey of the period will show grounds for deciding that, while a mechanical analysis or a social analysis may throw light on many aspects of Renaissance architecture, it is only an æsthetic analysis, and an æsthetic analysis in the strictest sense, which can render its history intelligible, or our enjoyment of it complete. If the essence, and not the accidents merely, of this architectural tradition is to be recognised, and some estimate of it obtained that does not wholly misconstrue its idea, this ground of analysis must be consistently maintained. The architecture of the Renaissance, we shall see reason to conclude, may be studied as a result of practical needs shaped by structural principle; it must be studied as an æsthetic impulsion, controlled by æsthetic laws, and only by an æsthetic criticism to be finally justified or condemned. It must, in fact, be studied as an art.

Here, however, is the true core of the difficulty. The science, and the history, of architecture are studies of which the method is in no dispute. But for the art of architecture, in this strict sense, no agreement exists. The reason has few problems so difficult as those which it has many times resolved. Too many definitions of architectural beauty have proved their case, enjoyed their vogue, provoked their opposition, and left upon the vocabulary of art their legacy of prejudice, ridicule, and confusion. The attempt to reason honestly or to see clearly in architecture has not been very frequent or conspicuous; but, even where it exists, the terms it must employ are hardened with misuse, and the vision it invokes is distorted by all the preconceptions which beset a jaded argument. Not only do we inherit the wreckage of past controversies, but those controversies themselves are clouded with the dust of more heroic combats, and loud with the battle-cries of poetry and morals, philosophy, politics, and science. For it is unluckily the fact that thought about the arts has been for the most part no more than an incident in, or a consequence of, the changes which men's minds have undergone with regard to these more stimulating and insistent interests. Hardly ever, save in matters of mere technique, has architecture been studied sincerely for itself. Thus the simplest estimates of architecture are formed through a distorting atmosphere of unclear thought. Axioms, holding true in provinces other than that of art, and arising historically in these, have successively been extended by a series of false analogies into the province of architecture; and these axioms, unanalysed and mutually inconsistent, confuse our actual experience at the source.

To trace the full measure of that confusion, and if possible to correct it, is therefore the first object of this book. We enter a limbo of dead but still haunting controversies, of old and ghostly dogmatisms, which most effectively darken the counsel of critics because their presence is often least perceived. It is time that these spectres were laid, or else, by whatever necessary libations of exacter thinking, brought honestly to life.

The path will then be clear to attempt, with less certainty of misconception, a statement of the æsthetic values on which Renaissance architecture is based.

To follow, in concrete detail, this Architecture of Humanism, to see how the principles here sketched out are confirmed by the practice of the Italian builders, and to trace their gradual discovery, may be the task of another volume.

ONE

Renaissance Architecture

The architecture of Europe, in the centuries during which our civilisation was under the sway of classical prestige, passed in a continuous succession through phases of extraordinary diversity, brevity and force. Of architecture in Italy was this most particularly true. The forms of Brunelleschi, masterful as they appeared when, by a daring reversion of style, he liberated Italian building from the alien traditions of the north, seem, in two generations, to be but the hesitating precursors of Bramante's more definitive art. Bramante's formula is scarcely asserted, the poise and balance of classic proportion is scarcely struck, before their fine adjustments are swept away upon the torrent that springs from Michael Angelo. In the ferment of creation, of which Italy from this time forth is the scene, the greatest names count, relatively, for little. Palladio, destined to provide the canon of English classic building, and to become, for us, the prime interpreter of the antique, here makes but a momentary stand among the contending creeds. His search for form, though impassioned, was too reactionary, his conclusions too academic and too set, for an age when creative vigour was still, beyond measure, turbulent. With that turbulence no art that was not rapid and pictorial in its appeal could now keep pace. The time was past when an architecture of such calculated restraint as Sammichele had foreshadowed could capture long attention; and the art of Peruzzi, rich though it was with never-exhausted possibilities, seems to have perished unexplored, because, so to say, its *tempo* was too slow, its interest too unobtrusive. Vignola, stronger perhaps than these, is before long forgotten in Bernini. Architecture becomes a debatable ground between the ideals of structure and decoration, and from their fertile conflict new inventions are ever forthcoming to please a rapidly-tiring taste. Fashions die; but the Renaissance itself, more irresistible than any force which it produced, begets its own momentum, and passes on, with almost the negligent fecundity of nature, self-destructive and self-renewing.

We are confronted with a period of architecture at once daring and pedantic, and a succession of masters the orthodoxy of whose professions is often equalled only by the licence of their practice. In spite of its liberty of thought, in spite of its keen individualism, the Renaissance is yet an age of authority; and Rome, but pagan Rome this time, is once more the arbiter. Every architect confesses allegiance to the antique; none would dispute the inspiration of Vitruvius. For many the dictates of the Augustan critic have the validity of a papal deliverance upon a point of faith. Yet their efforts to give expression to this seemingly identical enthusiasm are contradictory in the extreme. Never were the phases of a single art more diverse. For to consistency the Renaissance, with all its theories, was vitally indifferent. Its energy is at every moment so intense that the forms, not of architecture alone, but of every material object of common use, are pressed into simultaneous and sympathetic expression; yet it is guided on no sure or general course. Its greater schemes too often bear evidence to this lack of continuity, this want of subordination to inherited principle. Upon the problem of St. Peter's were engaged the minds of Bramante, Michael Angelo, Raphael, Peruzzi, Sangallo, Fontana, Maderna and Bernini. So much originality could not, without peril, be focussed at a single point; and those of Bramante's successors who were fortunate enough to carry their schemes into execution, obscured, if they did not ignore, the large idea which he had bequeathed to them. The history of St. Peter's is typical of the period. Shaped by a desire as powerful as it is undefined, its inventive impulse remains unexhausted, and style succeeds to style in the effort to satisfy the work-

ings of an imagination too swift and restless to abide the
fulfilment of its own creations. In this the Renaissance
stands alone. The mediæval Gothic had indeed been
equally rapid, and equally oblivious of its past, so rapid
and so oblivious that few of its principal buildings were
completed in the style in which they were begun. Nevertheless it pursued one undeviating course of constructive
evolution. Beside this scientific zeal the achievement of
the Italian builders might appear, at first sight, to be as
confused in aim as it was fertile in invention. Contrast it
with the cumulative labour, the intensive concentration,
by which the idea of Greek architecture, ever reiterated,
was sharpened to its perfection, and the Renaissance in
Italy seems but a pageant of great suggestions. Set it beside the antique styles of the East, compare it with the
monumental immobility which for eighteen centuries was
maintained in the architectural tradition of Egypt, and it
might pass for an energy disquieted and frivolous. Yet, at
every instant in the brief sequence of its forms, it is powerful and it is convinced; and from the control of its influence
Europe has attempted to free itself in vain.

We shall seek without success, among conditons external to art, for causes adequate to an effect so varied, so
violent, and so far-reaching. The revolutions which architecture underwent in Italy, from the fifteenth to the eighteenth century, corresponded to no racial movements; they
were unaccompanied by social changes equally sudden, or
equally complete; they were undictated, for the most part,
by any exterior necessity; they were unheralded by any new
or subversive discovery whether in the science of construction or in the materials at its command. All these, and
other such conditions, did indeed contribute to the architectural result. Sometimes they set their limits to what was
accomplished, sometimes they provided its opportunity.
But none of them separately, nor all in conjunction, will
sufficiently explain the essential character of the whole
movement, or of each successive step, nor afford any clue
to the sequence of its stages. They are like the accidents

of a landscape which might shape the course of a wandering stream. But the architecture of Italy is a river in the flood. Race, politics, the changes of society, geological facts, mechanical laws, do not exhaust the factors of the case. Taste—the disinterested enthusiasm for architectural form—is something which these cannot give and do not necessarily control. Nevertheless, it is by reference to these external factors that the architectural forms of the Renaissance are persistently explained.

Let us see how far such explanations can carry us. It is probably true that a 'Renaissance' of architecture in Italy was, on racial grounds, inevitable. Already in the twelfth century there had been a false dawn of classic style. Indeed, it seems evident that mediæval art could exercise but a temporary dominion among peoples who, however little of the authentic Roman strain they might legitimately boast, yet by the origin of their culture stood planted in Roman civilisation. Classic forms in Italy were indigenous and bound to reappear. And this fact is important. It enables us to dismiss that unintelligent view of Renaissance architecture, once fashionable, and still occasionally put forward, which regards it as a pedantic affectation, or perverse return to a manner of building that was alien and extinct. But it is a fact which in no way helps us to understand the precise form of classic culture which the Renaissance assumed. It does not explain the character, number, and variety of its phases. And it tells nothing of classic culture in itself. Racial considerations are here too general and too vague.

The field of politics might seem more fruitful. The growth of the new style is undoubtedly associated, at Florence, Milan, Naples and other city states, with the rise to power of the Italian 'tyrants,' themselves another echo of antiquity, and another characteristic expression of the Renaissance, with its cult for individuality and power. Cosimo the Great, whom Michelozzo followed into exile at Venice, Lorenzo, the protector of Giuliano da Sangallo, Alphonso in the South, in the North the Sforzas—these, and others like them, were certainly influential patrons. But it would be difficult to maintain that they left a deep imprint of themselves, or their government, upon the char- acter of the art. Gismondo Malatesta, tyrant of Rimini, the rough soldier who caused a Gothic church to be con- verted into the equivalent of a pagan temple dedicated to his mistress, and flanked it with the entombed bones of Greek philosophers and grammarians, may well impress us with his individuality; but, as between him and Alberti, his architect, himself of noble family and one of the greatest humanists of his time, there can be little doubt where the paramount imagination lay. The influence of patronage on art is easily mis-stated. Art may be brought to the service of the state and its rulers; but the most that rulers can do towards determining the *essence* of an art is to impose upon it a distinctively courtly character, and the coherence which comes of a strongly centralised organisation. We should, for instance, misconstrue the inmost nature of Augustan art, or of the art of Louis xiv., if we were to ignore this factor. But nothing similar is true of the Ren- aissance city-state. Here the conditions were merely such as to give free play to an architecture which, intrinsically, in its character as an art, remained independent of them. The sole centralising influence, in any imaginative sense, was that of the Church, and even this was not felt as such till after the art had acquired its own natural momentum in the free, secular life of Florence.

It must be recognised, however, that the existence, in the sixteenth century papacy, of a soil perfectly suited to receive the roots of the restored art was in itself a piece of rare good fortune. The return to the antique, however ten- tative and, so to say, provincial, at the first, was in essence and by implication a return to the 'grand style'—to an im- perial, and, in the literal sense, a 'catholic' architecture. For the assertion and development of such a style the papacy was the ideal instrument: the papacy with its im- perial court, its boast of ancient continuities, its claim to universal dominion, its pagan inheritance, and its pomp.

All such realities were favourable to the vigour of a partly retrospective enthusiasm, fascinated by the broken ruins in which ancient Rome had embodied splendours so similar to these. And this was not all. For, in proportion as the classic movement was no empty revival, in proportion as it represented a rising to the surface of the preferences, still vital and potent, of an ancient and indigenous culture, which claimed a future as confidently as it possessed the past, just in that measure it required a field in which to realise its own creative resources, its own untried originality. It could not have found itself in any rigid discipline or imposed continuity such as that which, later, in the France of Louis xiv., gave to architecture a formal and restricted aim. It needed the patronage of a large idea, but it required also space and scope, that it might attempt every mode of self-realisation yet stand committed to none. This space, and this patronage, the papacy was fitted to provide. The rivalry of successive popes, their diverse origins and sympathies, their common passion to leave behind them an enduring monument of their power; above all, their detached office, controlling the different states of Italy and forcing each of them to bring its own artistic temperament within the spell of Rome, gave architecture, in perfect combination, the focus and the liberty, the varied impulse and the renewed vitality necessary for making a great imaginative experiment under the influence of the antique.

The papacy, then, may be considered to have predetermined in some degree the formation of Renaissance style. Yet we must not exaggerate its contribution. By its imperial quality it will appear to have furnished the large idea to which the new classic architecture might stand in service. But we must not overlook the extent to which the papacy was itself indebted, for that quality, to the artists of the Renaissance. It is a common fallacy to account for artistic expression by external conditions for whose very being that expression is in some cases responsible, and which, but for that expression, would never, perhaps, have been supposed to exist. In the present case, no doubt, this point could not be pressed very far. Yet St. Peter's and the Vatican, and the great monuments of restored Rome, are witnesses no less to the power of architecture to create and define the imaginative value of the Renaissance papacy, than to the encouragement and inspiration which the papacy contributed to art. Moreover, the character of the papacy in this period was largely formed by the character of its popes; and such men as Pius II., Leo X., and Julius II., were fit patrons of Renaissance architecture, partly for the reason that they were cultivated enthusiasts, awake to the ideals of an art which, quite independently of themselves, had given evidence of its nature, and which was already, in the eyes of all men, an energy so vigorous and splendid, that the popes could conceive no securer means of adding to their fame than by inviting its support.

So, too, with the more particular religious and social movements by which the phases of Renaissance architecture have sometimes been explained. When the Counter-Reformation made its bid for popularity, it erected on every hand churches in the baroque manner frankly calculated to delight the senses and kindle common enthusiasms. Never, perhaps, has architecture been more successfully or more deliberately made the tool of policy than by this brilliant effort which transformed the face of Italy; nor has the psychological insight of the Jesuits been manifested with greater sureness than when it thus enlisted in the service of religion the most theatrical instincts of mankind. But, once more, the very success of the movement was occasioned by the fact, so well appreciated by the Jesuits, that the taste for such an architecture was already there. The readiness of the *seicento* Italians to respond to an architectural appeal, their delight in such qualities as these baroque churches embodied, are pre-existent facts. The achievement of the Jesuits lay in converting these preferences of a still pagan humanity to Catholic uses, aggressively answering the ascetic remonstrance of the Reformation by a still further concession to mundane senses. The artistic significance of the style which the Jesuits employed, remains something wholly independent of the uses to which they put it. To explain the first by the second is to misconstrue the whole matter. To condemn the first on account of the second, as has repeatedly been done, is nothing less than childish.

Somewhat similar objections will apply when the architectural history of Italy is interpreted as the outcome of social changes. The 'increase of wealth,' the 'rise of great families,' the 'luxurious habits of a more settled society'—those useful satellites of architectural history—helped, no doubt, to create the demand which architecture satisfied. But the significant point is precisely that it was to artistic uses that this wealth, this power, and these opportunities, were devoted, and to artistic uses of a particular kind. Rich and flourishing societies have not seldom grown up, and are growing up in our own time, without any corresponding result. Prosperity is a condition of great achievements; it is not their cause. It does not even stand in any fixed relation to their progress. It provides power, but does not, artistically, control its use. The economic conditions which, in Italy, assisted the architecture of the Renaissance to assume such prominence, did not vary with the marked and swift alterations of its style. The style had an orbit, and an impetus, of its own. In Italy nothing is commoner than to find an architectural display wholly disproportionate, and even unrelated, to the social purpose it ostensibly fulfils, and to the importance or prosperity of the individuals or communities responsible for its existence. Princely gates, more imposing than those of a great mansion, lift up their heads in the loneliest places of the Campagna, but nothing glorious goes in. They lead, and have always led, to unpeopled pastures or humble farmsteads. The baroque spirit delighted in this gay inconsequence. It appreciated grandeur for its own sake, æsthetically; and it had a sense of paradox. In Tuscany, on the other hand, though Cosimo had to rebuke the too lordly schemes of Brunelleschi, and though the Strozzi Palace frowns in unfinished grandeur, the noblest occasions are often met by an exquisite humility of architecture. Yet, chastened as it was to its extreme refinement, this modest style of Tuscany must sometimes have formed the frame to very mediæval manners. A great critic, Professor Wölfflin, reviewing the numerous changes in style which marked the entrance of the Baroque, is content to refer them to a change in 'the Spirit of the time.' Nineteenth century mythology is favourable to the phrase; and 'the Spirit of the time' is often spoken of as a social power. But 'the Spirit of the time' does not exist independently of the activities which manifest it. It is the atmosphere which results from their combined operation; or it is the influence of the earlier and more spontaneous of these activities as felt by those which come more tardily or more reluctantly into play. Now, among those activities, art and architecture were in Italy ever to the forefront, as spontaneous and vital a preoccupation as existed in the national life. It is hardly philosophical, among a number of parallel manifestations of energy, to explain the stronger by the weaker; yet that is what an appeal to 'the Spirit of the time,' if it means anything, here implies. When, therefore, we have interpreted a change in architecture by a change in 'the Spirit of the time' we have in this case demonstrated a mere tautology.

Nor shall we fare much better in the attempt to find the key to Renaissance architecture in constructive science. There have been occasions when the discovery of a new structural principle, or the use of a new material, has started architectural design upon a path which it has followed, as it were of necessity, unable to desist from its course until the full possibilities of the innovation had been explored. Each step is determined by a scientific logic; and beauty lingers in the art by a fortunate habit, or comes, in some new form, by accident to light. Such, in some sense, was the case with the mediæval Gothic; and so it might be with some future architecture of steel. But such was not the case with the architecture of the Italian Renaissance. No constructive innovation explains the

34

course which it pursued. The dome of Brunelleschi, unquestionably, by its audacity and grandeur, the effective starting-point of the Renaissance, was indeed a great triumph of engineering skill; but it involved no fundamental principle which was not already displayed in the dome of Pisa or the Baptistery of Florence. On the contrary, although the construction of the Renaissance was often vast in extent and courageous in conception, it was at the same time simpler and less scientific than that of the centuries immediately preceding, and it was based for the most part upon the simplest traditional Roman forms. In proportion, moreover, as the use of stucco became prevalent, the construction which it concealed became an object of indifference.

The one constructional practice which distinguishes the Renaissance does but confirm the insignificant interest which construction, as such, possessed for the men of this period. That practice is the constant and undisguised use of the tie-rod to strengthen and secure arches and vaults which of themselves were insufficient to withstand the outward thrusts. This was an expedient by no means unknown to the Gothic builders. But what in mediæval construction had been an exceptional remedy, was accepted by the Renaissance builders as an obvious and legitimate resource. There was nothing novel in the expedient. Its frequent recurrence signifies not the adoption of a new constructive principle, but the adoption of a new artistic point of view. The suggestive point about its use is that the element on which, in real fact, the stability of the construction depended was ignored, frankly and courageously, in the æsthetic design. The eye was expected to disregard it as completely as it disregards the prop which in ancient sculpture supports a prancing horse. That is to say, between the æsthetic purpose of the work, and the means by which, in actual construction, it could be realised, a sharp distinction was now admitted. How far such a distinction between construction and design is legitimate for architecture is open to dispute. The question, which is a difficult one, must be examined more closely in a later chapter. Here we may notice it merely as a confirmation of our statement, that it was not from any new constructive interest that the impulse of the Renaissance style was derived, or its progress defined. On the contrary, it is frequently objected that the decorative use of the Orders so conspicuous in Renaissance architecture did *not* express structure, that it was contrary to construction, and, for that reason, vicious.

Lastly, architectural design was not dictated, except to a slight degree, by the materials employed. This physical explanation of style is much favoured by modern critics, but it is singularly inapplicable to the period we are considering. Italy is rich in every kind of building material, and the architect could suit his needs. No doubt the great blocks of stone which could be quarried at Fiesole assisted the builders of the Pitti Palace, as it had assisted the Etruscans before them. Probably the inspiration lay rather in the Etruscan tradition than in the material itself. Still, had the Florentine builders rested content with the Etruscan masonry, it might be said, without essential untruth, that their materials determined their style. But the Florentines brought to perfection not only the most massive of Italian styles, but also the lightest. Their most remarkable achievement was a sudden power of quiet delicacy and grace. Conversely, when the baroque architects of Rome desired a monumental and Cyclopean effect, they obtained it without the Florentines' advantages. Again, the smooth *pietra serena* of Tuscany may lend itself to fine carving; but the passion of the Florentines for exquisite detail is no less marked in their painting, where no such factors operated, than in their architecture. Clearly, therefore, it sprang in both cases from an independent and native preference of taste. And, conversely, once more, the rough travertine of Rome did not yield up its 'natural' effect, its breadth of scale and roundness of feeling, until the baroque imagination, trained in painting to seek for soft transitions and broad shadow, began to require those qualities in architecture. Till then, travertine had been used, against its nature, in the Florentine tradition of sharp detail. In the Renaissance the imagination came first; and where it existed it never failed to find materials for its expression. No doubt one material was better than another, and an architect accustomed, as were the Italians, to his tools, would take the best he could; but the men of the Renaissance were notoriously, and perhaps viciously, indifferent to the matter. If they conceived a design which called for a material difficult to obtain, they made no scruple about imitating it. Their marbles and their stones are often of painted stucco. When the blocks of masonry with which they built were not in scale with the projected scheme, the real joints were concealed and false ones were introduced.[1] And these practices were by no means confined, as is sometimes suggested, to the later and supposedly decadent phases of the art. Material, then, was utterly subservient to style.

Enough has now perhaps been said to suggest that Renaissance architecture in Italy pursued its course and assumed its various forms rather from an æsthetic, and, so to say, internal impulsion than under the dictates of any external agencies. The architecture of the Renaissance is pre-eminently an architecture of Taste. The men of the Renaissance evolved a certain architectural style, because they liked to be surrounded by forms of a certain kind. These forms, as such, they preferred, irrespective of their relation to the mechanical means by which they were produced, irrespective of the materials out of which they were constructed, irrespective sometimes even of the actual purposes they were to serve. They had an immediate prefer-

[1] *e.g.* in the Strozzi Palace many apparently vast blocks of stone are made up of shorter ones with concealed vertical joints. In the Cancelleria, conversely, long stones are made to appear shorter than they are, by 'joints,' which are in reality only channels on the surface. In both cases the purpose is to maintain 'scale'; the unit of design, that is to say, is not material but æsthetic.

ence for certain combinations of mass and void, of light and shade, and, compared with this, all other motives in the formation of their distinctive style were insignificant. For these other motives, being accidental, exerted no consistent pressure, and, consequently, were absorbed or thrust aside by the steady influence of a conscious taste for form. As an architecture of taste, then, we must let it rest, where our historians are so unwilling to leave it, or where, leaving it, they think it necessary to condemn: as though there were something degraded in liking certain forms for their own sake and valuing architecture primarily as the means by which they may be obtained.

What is the cause of this prejudice? What is the reason of the persistent attempt to force upon architectural art such external standards, and to explain it by such external influences? Clearly, it is this. Taste is supposed to be a matter so various, so capricious, so inconsequent, and so obscure that it is considered hopeless to argue about it in its own terms. Either, it is thought, we must resign ourselves to chaos, or we must exclude taste from our discussion, or we must reduce taste to terms of something more constant and reliable. Only by so reducing it can we control it, or hope to understand it. The tendency, in fact, springs from the impatience of the intellect in the presence of a factor which seems to disown its authority, and to be guided, if it is guided at all, by instincts of which the intellect can give no immediate account. It is an unconscious attempt to drill art into the ready-made categories which we have found useful in quite other fields, and to explain the unfamiliar by the familiar. It is the application to art of the methods of science, which sometimes are less concerned with the ultimate truth about its facts than with bringing them within the range of a given intellectual formula. But it is unscientific to persist in the application when it is clear that the formula does not fit.

We have dealt in this chapter with a point of historical fact. It is historically true that the distinctive control in Renaissance architecture lay not in construction or materials or politics, but, chiefly and typically, in the taste for form. It follows that it is reasonable to analyse the Italian styles primarily in terms of taste: to ask, how far do they fulfil that third 'condition of well-building' which Wotton names 'delight.'

But it is one thing to state how Renaissance architecture arose; it is quite another to estimate its value. For it may be rejoined that good taste in architecture consists in approving what is truthfully built—expressive alike of the methods and materials of its construction on the one hand, and, on the other, of the ends it has to serve; and that if the taste of the Renaissance was indifferent to these points it was bad taste, and the architecture which embodied it bad architecture. Thus, the very factors which, on the point of *history*, we have relegated to a secondary place, might still, on the point of *æsthetics*, resume their authority.

This view of architecture has many adherents. It finds confirmation—so at least it is claimed—in the greater styles of the past, in the practice of the Greek and Gothic builders. To ignore this rejoinder would be to fall into the common error of dogmatic criticism, and to neglect a large part of actual artistic experience. But it is a view of architecture which the Renaissance builders, at least, were far from holding. It is at variance with buildings which were enjoyed, and enjoyed enthusiastically, by a people devoted, and presumably sensitive, to art.

Confronted by those rival dogmatisms, how can we proceed? The natural course would be to examine the buildings themselves and take the evidence of our own sensations. Are they beautiful, or not? But on our sensations, after all, we can place no immediate reliance. For our sensations will be determined partly by our opinions and, still more, by what we look out for, attend to, and expect to find. All these preoccupations may modify our judgment at every turn, and interpose between us and the clear features of the art an invisible but obscuring veil. Before we put faith in our sensations, before we accept the verdict of others, it is necessary to examine, more closely than has yet been done, the influences by which contemporary opinion, in matters of architecture, is unwittingly surrounded and controlled.

TWO

The Romantic Fallacy

The Renaissance produced no theory of architecture. It produced treatises on architecture: Fra Giocondo, Alberti, Palladio, Serlio, and many others, not only built, but wrote. But the style they built in was too alive to admit of analysis, too popular to require defence. They give us rules, but not principles. They had no need of theory, for they addressed themselves to taste. Periods of vigorous production, absorbed in the practical and the particular, do not encourage universal thought.

The death of the Renaissance tradition should have enabled men, for the first time, to take a general view of its history, and to define its principles, if not with scientific exactness, at least without provinciality or bias. Of the causes which precluded them from so doing, the first was the prolonged ascendency of the Romantic Movement.

The Romantic Movement created in all the arts a deep unrest, prompting men to new experiments; and, following on the experiments, there came a great enlargement of critical theory, seeking to justify and to explain. So it was with the theory of architecture. How far, in this change of thought, has it been strengthened and enriched; how far encumbered and confused? A clear view of Renaissance architecture requires an answer to this question.

Although, in every department of thought, there are principles peculiar to it, necessary to its understanding, and with reference to which it should properly be approached, yet all the elements of human culture are linked in so close and natural a federation, that when one among them becomes predominant, the others are affected to an instantaneous sympathy, and the standards appropriate to the one are transferred, with however little suitability, to all.

Such, towards the close of the eighteenth century, was the case of the Romantic Movement, which, from being an enlargement of the poetic sensibility, came, in the course of its development, to modify the dogmas and control the practice of politics and of architecture. By the stress which it laid on qualities that belong appropriately to literature, and find place in architecture, if at all, then only in a secondary degree, it so falsified the real significance of the art that, even at the present time, when the Romantic Movement is less conspicuous in the creation of architecture, the fallacies we shall trace to it are still abundantly present in its criticism.

Romanticism may be said to consist in a high development of poetic sensibility towards the remote, as such. It idealises the distant, both of time and place; it identifies beauty with strangeness. In the curious and the extreme, which are disdained by a classical taste, and in the obscure detail which that taste is too abstract to include, it finds fresh sources of inspiration. It is most often retrospective, turning away from the present, however valuable, as being familiar. It is always idealistic, casting on the screen of an imaginary past the projection of its unfulfilled desires. Its most typical form is the cult of the extinct. In its essence, romanticism is not favourable to plastic form. It is too much concerned with the vague and the remembered to find its natural expression in the wholly concrete. Romanticism is not plastic; neither is it practical, nor philosophical, nor scientific. Romanticism is poetical. From literature it derives its inspiration; here is its strength; and here it can best express its meaning. In other fields—as in music— it has indeed attained to unimagined beauties; but always within certain limits and upon fixed conditions. For here, on a borrowed ground, if it fail to observe the laws which music, or architecture, or life, as concrete arts, may impose, then even that element of value with Romanticism introduced, becoming mute and ineffective, is sacrificed in the failure of the whole.

It would be a mistake to imagine that Romanticism was in any way a new force at the time when, with the French Revolution, its various manifestations came into such startling prominence as to require attention and receive a name. Any movement strong enough to become conspicuously dominant must long previously, it is safe to suppose have been latently operative. And, in architecture, although the Romantic Movement of the nineteenth century dealt the final death-blow to the tradition of the Renaissance, yet that tradition, it must not be forgotten, was itself a romantic movement. The cult of mediævalism, stimulated by the revival of ballad literature and by antiquarian novelists, is not more romanticist than the idealisation of antiquity, four centuries earlier, stimulated by the revival of classic poetry and the enthusiastic antiquarianism of Paduan scholars. Nor, for that matter, is it more romanticist than the neo-Greek architectural movement of the Hellenising emperors in antiquity itself. Why, then, it is natural to ask, should a motive which in the second and fifteenth centuries proved a source of strength, be regarded, in the nineteenth, as a disastrous weakness?

The reason is simple. Architecture is the art of organising a mob of craftsmen. This, the original meaning of the word, expresses an essential fact. You can pass, in poetry, at a leap from Pope to Blake, for the sleepiest printer can set up the most original remarks. But the conceptions of an architect must be worked out by other hands and other minds than his own. Consequently, the changes of style in architecture must keep pace with the technical progress of the crafts. And if, at the bidding of a romantic fashion, an abrupt change of style be attempted, then the technique and organisation required by the new ideal must not be more exacting than those employed by the existent art. For neither technique nor organisation can be called into being suddenly and at will.

For this reason the romantic return to mediævalism failed, where the classic revival succeeded. The latter was concerned to restore the space, proportion and coherence of abstract design; and these the individual architect like Brunelleschi might hope to provide. He asked less, not more, of his craftsmen. The resources of skill acquired during centuries of Gothic practice were, technically, more than sufficient for the new tasks. Imaginatively, his sculptors were already imbued with the new classicism. And if, when they carved a frieze, they still betrayed some Gothic fancy, it mattered little: the point lay less in what they carved than in where they carved it, and this he could determine and control. But in the nineteenth century these conditions were reversed. To recreate the mediæval vision was incongruous with men's life. The new ideal required a variety of skilled crafts that were irrecoverably lost, and the architect, with nothing but his scholarship, set out to restore a style that had never been scholarly.

The purpose of romanticism should have been the fusion of a poetical interest with the forms and principles of an existing art. Had the Romantic Movement complied, even in some degree, with the essential conditions, a genuine architectural style might have been created, formed, as it were, out of the materials of that which it superseded. In some directions, while the good sense of the eighteenth century still controlled the situation, this was indeed accomplished. For the first signs of the change had been innocent enough. In the middle of the eighteenth century, that romantic attitude, which later was to culminate in a wholly false æsthetic, can already be recognised in a certain restlessness and satiety with native and traditional forms, and in a tendency to take interest in remote kinds of art. One of the earliest indications of this spirit is the taste, prevalent at that time in French society, and imitated to a less degree in England and in Italy, for the art of China, which Eastern commerce and the missionary efforts

of the Jesuits had made known.[1] In this case no condition
of concrete art was offended. For one of the phases of Renaissance art, which will fall in due course to be examined,
was the translation into architectural language of our pleasure in rapid, joyous, and even humorous physical movements. In France, this phase was embodied in the art of
Louis xv. It was contemporary with the climax of that interest in the Chinese which, we have said, was an early instance of the romantic spirit. Now, in its predilection for
gay and tortuous forms, as also in its love of finish, the art
of China (as the French understood it) was perfectly congruous with their own. It required no organisation which
contemporary art was not able to supply; and the zeal for it
came at a time when architecture was so vigorous that it
readily assimilated such elements of the new material as
suited its requirements, and produced, in the *Chinoiseries*
of the eighteenth century, a charming invention, which,
while it gratified the romantic instinct of the age, added,
at the same time, to its appropriate decorative resources.

The successive stages of the Gothic taste exhibit very
clearly the character of romanticism, and the point at which
it overweighs the sense of form. Up to the middle of the
eighteenth century the mediæval style merely spelt discomfort, desolation, and gloom.[2] Noble owners, so far as
their purse allowed, converted their Gothic inheritances,
as best they could, to the Georgian taste, or rebuilt them
outright. Then enters the spirit of history, the romance

[1] The Chinese Trading Company of Colbert was founded
in 1660; the Compagnie des Indes in 1664. From 1698 to
1703 the *Amphitrite* cruised in Chinese water. *Vide J.*
Guérin, *Les Chinoiseries au XVIIIme Siècle.*

[2] There were not wanting those who maintained this opinion throughout the whole period of the romantic movement.
In 1831, when it was at its height, even the stately and tem-
pered mediævalism of Knole still inspires the Duchesse de
Dino with the utmost melancholy: 'Cette vieille fée (the
housekeeper) montre fort bien l'antique et lugubre demeure
de Knowles, dont la tristesse est incomparable.'—Duchesse de
Dino, *Chronique.*

of the distant and the past, with archæology at its heels. The connoisseurs, about 1740, are full of zeal for the stylistic distinctions between the Egyptian, the Gothic, and the Arabesque, and charmingly vague about their limits. Their studies are pursued without calling in question the superior fitness of the classical tradition. Nevertheless, the orthodoxies of archæology now hold sway. They are submitted to not without reluctance. Gray, in 1754, writes of Lord Brooke, at Warwick Castle: 'He has sash'd the great Appartment . . . and being since told that square sash-windows were not Gothic, he has put certain whim-wams within side the glass, which, appearing through, are made to look like fret-work. Then he has scooped out a little Burrough in the massy walls of the place for his little self and his children, which is hung with chintzes in the exact manner of Berkley Square or Argyle Buildings. What in short can a lord do nowadays that is lost in a great, old, solitary castle but skulk about, and get into the first hole he finds, as a rat would do in like case?' [3] But the vital taste of the time could not rest satisfied with archæology. The Gothic forms were a romantic material, rich with the charm of history. Could they be fused with the living style? Batty Langley thought they could, and by no other mind more readily than his own. 'Ancient architecture, restored and improved by a great variety of grand and useful designs, entirely new, in the Gothick mode'; 'Gothic Architecture, improved by rules and proportions.' These were the titles Langley successively affixed to the first two editions of his work. They show two alternative ways of regarding the same question—the Gothic, steadied and sobered by 'proportion'; the ancient architecture made various with Gothic fancies. Here was no question of a mediæval revival, as the next century understood it, but a true attempt at fusion. But then the two elements to be fused were utterly incongruous. If this was not clear before, Batty Langley's designs must have made it obvious to all who

[3] *Letters of Thomas Gray*, edited by D. C. Tovey, vol. 1. No. cxiv.

were not blinded by historical enthusiasm. And, on the whole, the right inference was drawn. 'Gothic Umbrellos to terminate a view'; Gothic pavilions for 'the intersection of ways in a Wood or Wildernesse,' were well enough. Here they might be admitted as curiosities—as literary reminders of the romantic past, or shrines to the poetry of nature with which the mediæval style was conceived to be related. Above all, they might act as a foil to the classical elements themselves, and do a dual service by stimulating the sense of history while they set off the immaculate consistency of the time. The Gothic suggestions might even penetrate the house. They might, without discordancy, provide the traceries of a book-case or enrich the mouldings of a Chippendale table. Here and there, in the light spirit of fashionable caprice, they might furnish the decoration of a room, just as, elsewhere, an Eastern scheme might dominate. But to go further and Gothicise the main design, seemed at the first an obvious fault of taste. 'I delight,' writes Gray to Wharton, 'to hear you talk of giving your house some Gothic ornaments already. If you project anything, I hope it will be entirely within doors: and don't let me (when I come gaping into Coleman Street) be directed to the "gentleman's at the ten pinnacles" or "with the Church Porch at his door." ' [4] And when, at Strawberry Hill, Horace Walpole allowed a quaint imitation of mediævalism to furnish his whole design, the concession, startling and even absurd as it seemed to his contemporaries, was made in a spirit of amused pedantry and conscious eccentricity, or, at most, of archæological patronage; nor could the amateurs of that time have credited the idea that the trefoils and pinnacles of Walpole's toy heralded a movement which would before long exterminate alike the practice and the understanding of their art. The irony of this situation has an exact and tragic counterpart in the favour accorded at that epoch by the more philosophic and enlightened of the French aristocracy to those theories of 'natural' equality (themselves another expression of ro-

[4] *Letters of Thomas Gray*, vol. i. No. cxiv.

manticism) which were destined to drive these noble patrons, their philosophy and their enlightenment, entirely
out of existence.

Side by side with this sense of Gothic as an amusing
exotic—an attitude which was thoroughly in the Renaissance spirit and characteristic, above all, of the eighteenth
century—there grew up a more serious perception of its
imaginative value. When Goethe visits Strasburg Cathedral
it is no longer, for him, the work of 'ignorant and monkish
barbarians,' but the expression of a sublime ideal: and
Goethe's mind foreshadows that of the coming century.
At the same time he has no quarrel with the existing standards; a complete reaction against these is as yet unimagina-
ble. But a change of attitude shows itself both with regard
to Gothic and also to the living style. These now came
more and more to be regarded *symbolically*, as standing
for certain ideas. And in particular the habit arose of regarding Greek and Gothic art as contrasted, parallel and
alternative modes of feeling. But the good taste of the
period, although already permeated with Romanticism, recognised this distinction between them: the Gothic must
remain an external object of admiration; the Greek feeling
could be fused with the existing art, the Greek forms
grafted on to, or extricated from, the living tradition. Just
as it had required no impossible change to impart a Chinese turn to the gay Renaissance style of Louis xv.,
so, with equal facility, the romantic idealisation of
Greece could be expressed by emphasising the elements of
severity in the essentially Renaissance style of Louis xvi.
But a species of literary symbolism becomes increasingly
evident in the attempt. *The interest is shifted, more and
more, from the art itself to the ideals of civilisation.* The
Greek modes of the period are deliberately meant to 'suggest' its political or other doctrines; and the intrusion of
Egyptian detail which followed Napoleon's African ex-
pedition is an instance of the same allusive tendency. Thus,
though an apparent continuity is still maintained, a radical
change has taken place. A romantic classicism of sentiment

and reflection has overlaid and stifled the creative classicism which sprang up in the *quattrocento* and till now had held control. In imparting to the Renaissance tradition this literary flavour, in adopting this unprecedentedly imitative manner, the vigour of the Renaissance style was finally and fatally impaired. In obedience to the cult of 'ideal' severity it cut down too scrupulously all evidence of life; and when, with the passing of the old order of society, vanished also the high level of workmanship and exquisite ordering of ideas which that society had exacted, then the ruin of the classical style was consummated, and poverty of execution completed what poverty of design had begun. The antique, which Brunelleschi invoked, was now realised with full self-consciousness; in the last stages of the Empire style the resources of classic architecture seem at length to be exhausted; in that style the architects of Napoleon built the monument, and wrote the epitaph, of Renaissance art.

But the romantic impulse, when it had thus dealt the death-blow to the living Renaissance tradition, still had its course to run. The attitude of mind of which the Empire style was the classical expression had yet to manifest itself in other forms less fit. Its final and definitive achievement was, of course, the general revival of Gothic. Towards this end the literary and sentimental currents of the time combined more and more powerfully to impel it, and as the nineteenth century progressed and the old standards became forgotten, romantic enthusiasm in architecture was concentrated upon this alone. Beckford, at Fonthill, finding in the Georgian mansion he inherited no adequate stimulus to the raptures of imagination, instructed his architect Wyatt to design 'an ornamental building which should have the appearance of a convent, be partly in ruins and yet contain some weatherproof apartments.'[5] The scheme

[5] Vide *The Life and Letters of William Beckford*, by L. Melville. Beckford rebuilt his tower, but it again fell to earth. His life (1760-1844) bridges the interval between Walpole and Ruskin, and is an admirable example of the romantic spirit at its height. *Vathek* and Fonthill exhibit its power and its weakness.

at length developed into vast proportions. Impressive galleries of flimsy Gothic delighted their master with vague suggestions of the Hall of Eblis, and a tower, three hundred feet in height, rose above them to recall the orgies of the wicked Caliph. Five hundred workmen laboured here incessantly, by day, and with torches in the night. But the wind blew upon it, and the wretched structure fell incontinently to the ground. The ideal of a monastic palace 'partly ruined' was ironically achieved. And the author of *Vathek*, contemplating in the torchlight his now crumpled, but once cloud-capped, pinnacles, may stand for the romantic failure of his time—for the failure of the poetic fancy, unassisted, to achieve material style.

It forms no part of our scheme to dwell upon the phases of the mediæval revival. They exhibit the romantic spirit in a cruder, a less interesting, and a less instructive manner than the Greek movement which we have been criticising. Technique, organisation, vigour, understanding—everything, in fact, save learning and enthusiasm, were wanting to it. It illustrates, as abundantly as one could wish, the effect upon architecture of an exculsively literary attitude of mind; and as few to-day would do otherwise than lament its achievements, we may take leave of them.

But among the consequences of that ill-timed experiment we have to emphasise this. The Romantic Movement, in destroying the existing architectural tradition, destroyed simultaneously the interest which was felt in its principles, and replaced it by a misunderstood mediævalism out of which no principles of value could ever be recovered. The catastrophe for style was equally a catastrophe for thought. To this, without doubt, no small part of the existing confusion in architectural criticism may be traced. We laugh at Fonthill and Abbotsford and Strawberry Hill: Georgian architecture once again enjoys its vogue. Yet the Romantic Tendency, expelled from architecture, still lingers in its criticism. The Gothic revival is past, while the romantic prejudices that engendered it remain. And these it is important to define.

The first fallacy of Romanticism, then, and the gravest, is to regard architecture as *symbolic*. Literature is powerful to invest with fascination any period of history on which its art is imaginatively expended. Under the influence, directly or indirectly, of literature the whole past of the race is coloured for us in attractive or repellent tones. Of some periods inevitably we think with delight; of others with distaste. A new historical perspective, a new literary fashion, may at any time alter the feeling we entertain. Yet the concrete arts which these different periods produced remain always the same, still capable of addressing the same appeal to the physical senses. If, then, we are to attend impartially to that permanent appeal, we must discount these 'literary' preconceptions. But everything which recalls a period of the past may recall, by association, the emotions with which that period is, at the time, poetically regarded. And to these emotions, orginally engendered by literature, romanticism makes the other arts subservient. The element in our consciousness which ought to be discounted, it makes paramount. Its interest in the arts is that, like poetry, they should bring the mind within the charmed circle of imaginative *ideas*. But these ideas really belong to the literary imagination whence they sprang, and one result of applying them to architecture, where they are not inherent, is that all permanence and objectivity of judgment is lost. Thus, for example, the Gothic building from being the 'expression' of 'ignorant and monkish barbarians,' came to 'suggest' the idealised Goth—'firm in his faith and noble in his aspirations'—who inspired the enthusiasm of Coleridge; and the forms of an architecture which later came to be admired as the lucid expression of constructive mathematics were about this time commonly praised as the architectural image of primeval forests. Some minds find in the work of the mediæval builders the record of a rude and unresting energy; others value it as the evidence of a dreaming piety. Now, it is an 'expression of infinity made imaginable'; next, the embodiment of 'inspired' democracy. It is clear that there is no limit to this kind of writing, and we have only to follow the romantic criticism through its diverse phases to feel convinced of its total lack of any objective significance. Any characteristic, real or imagined, of a mixed set of northern races, during a period of several hundred years, is discovered at will in these cathedrals of the twelfth and thirteenth centuries, although it is more than doubtful how far such characteristics are capable of being embodied in architecture, or, if embodied, how far we, with our modern habits of thought, can extract them unfalsified, or, if extracted, how far they are relevant to the quality of the work. The whole process is purely literary, its charm is in the literary value of the idea itself, or in the act and process of association. Moreover, since literary exercises invite effects of contrast, the architecture of the Renaissance comes to be treated, like the villain in the melodrama, as a mere foil to the mediæval myth. And because Renaissance life happened to yield no stimulus to the nineteenth century imagination, the architecture which ministered to the uses of that life became *ipso facto* commonplace. A combination of plastic forms has a sensuous value apart from anything we may *know* about them. Romanticism allows what it knows, or conceives itself to know, about the circumstances among which the forms were produced, to divert it from giving unbiassed attention to the purely æsthetic character, the sensuous value, of the concrete arts. If it is a question of architecture, the architectural design is taken as standing for the period which invented and is associated with it, and as suggesting, conventionally, the general imaginative state, the complex feelings of approval or disapproval which the idea of that period happens to evoke. Architecture, in fact, becomes primarily symbolic. It ceases to be an immediate and direct source of enjoyment, and becomes a mediate and indirect one.

Under the romantic influence, then, the interest in architecture is symbolic, and taste becomes capricious. But that is not all. It becomes also unduly stylistic, and unduly antiquarian. For in proportion an architectural form is symbolically conventional its precise character becomes far less important than its general so-called 'style'; just as in a handwriting the precise forms are less important than the meanings to which they refer, and exist only to call up the latter. Romanticism conceives styles as a stereotyped language. Nineteenth century criticism is full of this pre-possession: its concern is with styles 'Christian' and 'un-Christian'; one 'style' is suitable to museums and banks and cemeteries; another to colleges and churches; and this not from any architectural requirements of the case, but from a notion of the *idea* supposed to be suggested by a square battlement, a Doric pillar, or a pointed arch.[6] And such criticism is far more occupied with the importance of having, or not having, these features in general, than with the importance of having them individually beautiful, or beautifully combined. It sets up a false conception of style and attaches exaggerated value to it. For it looks to the conventional marks of historical styles for the sake of their symbolic value, instead of recognising style in general for its own value.

And there ensues a further error. Every period of romanticism, ancient or modern, has, it is safe to say, been a period of marked antiquarianism. The glamour of the past, and the romantic veneration for it, are very naturally extended to the minutiæ in which the past so often is preserved, and are bound to lend encouragement to their study. Nor is this study in itself other than beneficial. But the fault of the antiquarian spirit, in architectural thought, is precisely that it attaches an undue importance to detail as opposed to those more general values of Mass, Space, Line, and Coherence with which architecture properly deals, and which it will be the later purpose of this study to

[6] Nor is this prepossession extinct. When, recently, the most eminent of English architects projected a basilica for the Hampstead Garden Suburb, the Bishop of London swept the admirable scheme aside, declaring he 'must have a spire point to God.' We trust his lordship is finding some solace at Golder's Green for the signal injury done him by Sir Christopher Wren.

analyse and describe. For the present it is enough to emphasise the fact that between Renaissance architecture and the antiquarian criticism of the Romantic fallacy there is a fundamental opposition: and that opposition lies in their attitude to detail. For antiquarian criticism regards detail as the supreme consideration and Renaissance architecture regards it as a secondary and subservient consideration. And not only do they give it a different degree of importance, but, still more, they give it an importance of a wholly different kind. For in Renaissance architecture the purpose of detail, as we shall see, is primarily to give effect to the values of Mass, Space, Line, and Coherence in the whole design; and, secondarily, upon a smaller scale, to exhibit these qualities in itself. But for the romantic or antiquarian criticism it is required to be 'scholarly,' that is, to correspond exactly to some detail previously used in the period poetically approved. In this way, although it would seem highly unscholarly not to discover the æsthetic function of detail in general before dogmatising upon its use in particular cases, the antiquarian criticism of architecture has usurped the prestige of scholarship. And thus the romantic attitude which begins in poetry ends in pedantry, and the true spirit of architecture eludes it altogether. In the warfare of romantic controversy, Renaissance forms were defiantly multiplied, and sneeringly abused, as though the merit of the style consisted in the detached and unvalued elements common to the Piazzetta of Venice and the clubs of Pall Mall. Like the dishonoured fragments that mark the site of a forgotten temple, detail, mutilated by ignorant misuse—detail, and the conventional insignia of the styles—was all that remained of the broken edifice of a humanist tradition. And, as the merit of Renaissance architecture consists less in the variety than in the disposition of its forms, it became at last, as its enemies accused it of always having been, the lifeless iteration of a stereotyped material.

The first pitfall, therefore, into which architectural criticism fell was that prepared for it by the Romantic Movement. The understanding of Renaissance architecture suffered from this, and still suffers, both by neglect, and by misinterpretation. It was inevitable that Romantic criticism should neglect the Renaissance style. Its antiquarian enthusiasts found in it no free scope, because the field was already well explored, the subject well formulated: they were revolted, moreover, by the unconventional use which the Renaissance artists often made of classical design; and, attracted to the mediæval by its wealth of unexplored detail, they followed all the more willingly the summons of of the romantic impulse which, by an accident of culture, had now set towards the middle ages. Its poetic enthusiasts, equally, were repelled from the Renaissance tradition because it was insufficiently remote, insufficiently invested with the glamour of the unknown; because it could be made symbolic of no popular ideas, and because it could not, like the Greek or the Gothic, be fitted at once into a ready-made, poetical connection. And thus, insensibly, the Renaissance style, since symbolic it had to be, became symbolic of ideas that were unpopular. The conditions in which it had grown up seemed relatively prosaic. Prosaic, therefore, and dull the Renaissance forms must necessarily be found.[7]

[7] Cf. Mr. Lethaby in a recent work: 'It must, I think, be admitted by those who have in part understood the great primary styles, Greek or Gothic, that the Renaissance is a style of boredom. . . . Gothic art witnesses to a nation in training hunters, craftsmen, athletes; the Renaissance is the art of scholars, courtiers. . . .' Such a statement, in a history which is content to dismiss the whole period in eight pages (or rather less than is devoted to the architecture of Babylon), may justify us in saying that, at the hands of our romantically-minded critics, the Renaissance suffers from neglect, and that it suffers from misinterpretation. For Mr. Lethaby further complains of its buildings that they are 'architects' architecture'; architecture, that is to say, not convertible, presumably, into terms of poetry or historical romance, but requiring a knowledge of architectural principles for its appreciation. Renaissance architecture, in fact, is here read off in terms of Renaissance society, and those who enjoy it as an art are stig-

Such were the consequences of the prepossession which *translates* material forms into terms of 'literary' ideas. Yet it must not be said that literary ideas have no 'legitimate' place in architectural experience. Every experience of art contains, or may contain, two elements, the one direct, the other indirect. The direct element includes our sensuous experience and simple perceptions of form: the immediate apprehension of the work of art in its visible or audible material, with whatever values may, by the laws of our nature, be inherently connected with that. Secondly, and beyond this, there are the associations which the work awakens in the mind—our conscious reflections upon it, the significance we attach to it, the fancies it calls up, and which, in consequence, it is sometimes said to express. This is the indirect, or associative, element.

These two elements are present in nearly every æsthetic experience; but they may be very differently combined. Literature is an art which deals preponderatingly with 'expression.' Its appeal is made through the indirect element. Its emphasis and its value lie chiefly in the significance, the meaning and the associations of the sounds which constitute its direct material. Architecture, conversely, is an art which affects us chiefly by direct appeal. Its emphasis and its value lie chiefly in material and that abstract disposition of material which we call form. Neither in the one case nor in the other is the method wholly simple. Mere sound in poetry is an immediate element in its effect. And some visual impressions in architecture are bound up almost inextricably with elements of 'significance': as, for example, the sight of darkness with the notion of gloom, or of unbroken surfaces with the notion of repose. Nevertheless, the direct elements of poetry—its sound and form—

matised as 'architects.' When a critic, perhaps as learned and as eminent as any now writing on the subject of architecture in England, can offer us these censures, even in a popular work, as though they were accepted commonplaces, it is not easy to hope that the Romantic Fallacy is becoming extinct.— W. R. Lethaby, *Architecture*, 1912, pp. 232-33.

are valuable chiefly *as means to the significance*. They are employed to convey refinements of meaning, or to awaken trains of association, of which mere unassisted syntax is incapable. They enrich or sharpen our *idea*. The sounds delight us because, in them, the sense is heightened; and formal rhyme, by linking one phrase with another, adds a further intricacy of suggestion. But the merely formal, merely sensuous values of poetry are fully experienced when we read a poem in an unknown language; and the experiment should assure us that in literature the direct elements are valuable, almost solely, as a means to the indirect, and that the method of the art is strictly associative. In architecture, on the other hand, so small is here the necessary importance of mere significance, that a building whose utilitarian intention is crudely ignoble, and which is thus symbolic of ignoble things, may easily affect us, through its direct elements, as sublime. Literature may possess abstract architectural properties—scale, proportion, distribution—independent of its significance; architecture may evoke a poetic dream, independent of its forms; but, fundamentally, the language of the two arts is distinct and even opposite. In the one we await the meaning; in the other we look to an immediate emotion resulting from the substance and the form.

The reason of this difference is obvious. The material of literature is *already* significant. Every particle of it has been organised in order to convey significance, and in order to convey the same significance to all. But for the material of architecture, no system of accepted meanings has been organised. If, therefore, we derive associative values from its forms, those values will be determined wholly by the accidents of our time and personality. Our readings will disagree. Thus, while each individual, or generation, may add to the direct pleasures of architecture a further element of associative delight, this associative element is not fixed or organisable; it does not contain the true intention or typical value of the art, and cannot be fitted to contain them.

Now since language, meaning, and association play so large a part in our practical life, and form the very texture of our thought, there has been little danger at any time that the *significance* of literary art should be overlooked. There has never been—save perhaps to a slight degree in the eighteenth century—an 'architectural fallacy' in literature, though it has often been the case that the minor element of value—the sensuous element of literature—is totally forgotten. But this same habitual preoccupation with 'significance' which has kept literature vital has, in architecture, led us to lay undue weight on what is there the secondary element, and to neglect its direct value, its immediate and typical appeal. This, then, is the 'literary fallacy' in architecture. It neglects the fact that in literature meaning, or fixed association, is the universal term; while in architecture the universal term is the sensuous experience of substance and of form.

The Romantic Movement is a phase, precisely, of this literary preoccupation. It is the most extreme example of the triumph of association over direct experiences which the history of culture contains. Its influence upon taste can never be quite undone; nor need we wish it. Romanticism, as a conscious force, has brought with it much that is valuable, and holds the imagination of the age with an emphatic and pervasive control. But the danger is great lest a spirit which has rendered intelligible so many ancient and forgotten beauties, and created so many that are new, may, in its impetus, render ineffective for us some less insistent types of art, towards the perfection of which the tradition of centuries has austerely worked. Such an art is the architecture of the Renaissance. Here, then, if we indulge at all in literary ideas, let us at least be sure that they do not obscure from us the value of the style.

One fact should be stated in defence. These 'literary' ideas ought not to be the *primary* value of a material art; they are, nevertheless, its *ultimate* value. For, since man is a self-conscious being, capable of memory and association, all experiences, of whatever kind, will be merged, after they have been experienced, in the world of recollection—will become part of the shifting web of ideas which is the material of literary emotion. And this will be true of architectural experience. It may begin as a sensuous perception, but as such it is necessarily more transient and occasional than its remembered significance, and more isolated and particular than when fused by reflection with the rest of our remembered life. Its significance outlives it in the mind. There is, therefore, so to say, a literary background to the purely sensuous impression made upon us by plastic form, and this will be the more permanent element in our experience. When we renew the sensuous perception of the work of art, in addition to the immediate value this perception may have for us, there will be, surrounding it, a penumbra of 'literary' and other values. And as our attention to the sensuous properties relaxes, it is to these that it will naturally turn. In so far, then, as the literary values of the work of art enrich our complete experience of it, they are clear gain. And in so far as the Romantic Movement has stimulated our sensibility to such literary values, that also is a clear gain. It would be absurd to demand (as in some of the arts enthusiasts are constantly demanding) that we should *limit* our enjoyment of an art to that delight which it is the peculiar and special function of the art to provide. To sever our experience into such completely isolated departments is to impoverish it at every point. In the last resort, as in the first, we appreciate a work of art not by the single instrument of a specialised taste, but with our whole personality. Our experience is inevitably inclusive and synthetic. It extends far beyond the mere reaction to material form. But its nucleus, at least, should be a right perception of that form, and of its æsthetic function. It is reasonable, then, to claim that the æsthetic enjoyment which is proper and special to a given art should be the first and the necessary consideration, and that in relation to this the quality of a style should primarily be appraised. Whether or not that peculiar enjoyment can be enriched and surrounded with others of a different and more general nature must be a secondary question, and one with which the criticism of a given art, as such, need have no concern. When, therefore, our architectural critics condemn the Renaissance style on this secondary ground before they have fairly considered its claims on the primary ground, this, we may fairly say, is unsound and misleading criticism, criticism tending to obscure real values and diminish possible enjoyments, criticism vitiated by the Romantic Fallacy.

THREE

The Romantic Fallacy (*continued*)
Naturalism and the Picturesque

1   Romanticism has another aspect. We have seen that it allows the poetic interest of distant civilisation to supplant the æsthetic interest of form. But the romantic impulse is not attracted to history alone. It is inspired by the distant and the past; but it is inspired, also, by Nature. For, obviously, those qualities which romanticism seeks, these Nature possesses in the highest degree. Nature is strange, fantastic, unexpected, terrible. Like the past, Nature is remote. Indifferent to human preoccupations and disowning human agency, Nature possesses all the more forcibly an imaginative appeal. Thus, in the last century and earlier, together with the ballad-revival and the historical fiction, came, far more powerful than either, a new poetry of Nature. Under the influence of this poetry, Nature's unconsidered variety became the very type and criterion of beauty, and men were led by an inevitable consequence to value what is various, irregular, or wild, and to value it wherever it might be found. As in the cult of the past, so, too, in this cult of the 'natural,' it was literature, the true instrument of the Romantic Movement, that led the way.

It is evident that architecture and the criticism of architecture have reflected this poetic change. The formal garden, necessarily, was the first object of attack. In the Renaissance taste the garden was an extension of the main design. It was a middle term between architecture and Nature. The transition from house to landscape was logically effected by combining at this point formality of design with naturalness of material. The garden was thus an integral, an architectural, element in the art. But when Nature, through poetry, acquired its prestige, the formal garden stood condemned. Unpleasing in itself, because 'unnatural,' it was in addition a barbarous violence, a ruthless vandalism upon pools and trees. It was an offence against Nature all the more discordant because it was expressed in Nature's terms. Thus, before the impact of Naturalism shook traditional design in actual architecture, the formal garden was already gone. Eighteenth century philosophers, seated under porticoes still impeccably Greek, were enabled comfortably to venerate Nature—or, if not Nature, at least her symbol—as they watched their ancestral but unromantic gardens give place to a 'prospect' of little holes and hills. At their bidding a change was wrought throughout Europe, as sudden as it was complete. In a moment every valley had been dejected, the straight made crooked, and the plain places rough.

The change in architecture was not slow to follow. Here, as the last chapter showed, a romantic sense of history, treating styles as symbols, could look with equal favour on the Gothic and the Greek, and had provoked a romantic revival of both. But the romantic sense of Nature weighted the balance in favour of the mediæval. The Gothic builders belonged to the 'nobly savage' north, and had built against a background of forest and tempest. The Greeks stood for reason, civilisation, and calm. More than this, a certain 'natural' quality belonged to the Gothic style itself. Like Nature, it was intricate and strange; in detail realistic, in composition it was bold, accidental and irregular, like the composition of the physical world. Among the causes of the Gothic revival, the poetry of Nature, that cast on all such qualities its transforming light, may certainly be given an important place.

The influence of the sense of Nature upon building did not exhaust itself in the taste for Gothic. In England there grew up a domestic architecture which attaches itself to no historic style and attempts no definite design. It is applied, like the Georgian manner before it, indifferently to the cottage and the great house. But while the Georgian taste sought to impart to the cottage the seemly distinction of the manor, the modern preference is to make the manor share in the romantic charm of the cottage. In Latin countries this architecture is not found; its place is wholly taken by a resurrection of the 'Styles.' But in England, where the hold of style is slighter and the sentiment of landscape more profound, the rustic influence in taste has been extreme. It favours an architecture which satisfies practical convenience, and, for the rest, relies on a miscellany of sloping roofs and jutting chimneys to give a 'natural' beauty to the group. Save for a certain choice in the materials and some broad massing of the composition, the parts bear no relation to one another or to the whole. No such relation is attempted, for none is desired. The building grows, without direction, from the casual exigencies of its plan. The effect intended, if not secured, is wholly 'natural.' The house is to take the colour of the countryside, to lie hidden in the shadows and group itself among the slopes. Such in fairness is its ideal, realised too seldom. So far as this architecture takes any inspiration from the past, it looks to the old farm-buildings long lived in, patched, adapted, overgrown: buildings, so unconscious in their intent, so accidental in their history, as almost to form part of the Nature that surrounds them, and for whose service they exist.

What measure of beauty may belong to such an architecture will later be considered. It is irrelevant here to insist on the unfortunate effect it is calculated to produce when reiterated, with how monotonous a variety, on either side of a continuous street. But certainly, whatever be its merits, the habit of taste which it implies is hardly favourable to an understanding of the Renaissance. Order and subtleties of proportion require an habitual training in the eye. The Greeks, as some of the 'optical' corrections of the Parthenon have revealed, responded here to distinctions of which to-day even a practised taste will be almost insensible. The Renaissance inherited their ideal, if not their delicacy of sense. But a 'natural' architecture, so far from affording such practice to the eye, raises a prejudice against order itself; because whatever qualities a 'natural' architecture may possess are dependent on the negation of order. A taste formed upon this violent and elementary variousness of form, conceives a Renaissance front as a blank monotony because that, by contrast, is all it can discern. What wonder, then, if it accepts the verdict of the poetry of Nature, and declares the Renaissance style to be a weary and contemptible pomp, while it endows its own incompetence with the natural 'dignity' of the fields and woods.

Two duties, then, were required of architecture when the poetry of Nature had done its work. First, it must disguise, or in some way render palatable, the original sin of its existence: the fact that it was an artificial thing, a work of man, made with hands. To this end Nature herself might seem to have intended a variety of creeping, and ultimately overwhelming, plants, by means of which much of the architectural art of England has been successfully rendered vain.[1] To eradicate the intellectual element of design, to get rid of the consistent thought which means formality, is thus the first or negative condition of a 'natural' architecture. Its second aim is more positive. When once the evil spirit of conscious art has been exorcised, the door can be opened to a pandemonium of romance. The poetry of Nature can infect architecture with all her moods: idyllic in the rustic style we have described; fantastic and wild in every kind of mediæval reminiscence or modern German eccentricity.

[1] The habit of smothering fine architecture in vegetation is peculiarly English. The chapel of Trinity College at Oxford— to take an example out of a thousand—is habitually indicated to visitors as an object of special admiration *on account of* a crude red creeper which completely conceals it, together with the fact that it is, or would be, one of the most graceful works of architecture in that city. *Naturam furca expellas.* . . . But our romantic professors have evidently abandoned the struggle and exchanged Horace for Wordsworth.

It is of the essence of romantic criticism that it permits literary fashion to control architectural taste. This is the cardinal point to which once more we are brought back, and on which once more we may insist. That the architectural judgment is made in unconsciousness of the literary bias is immaterial. A literary fashion is easily conceived of as an absolute truth, and the unconsciousness of a prejudice only adds to its force. For the power of literature extends far beyond its conscious students; by a swift contagion it determines, even in illiterate minds, the channels of their thought, the scope of their attention, and the values to which they will respond. It leads men to say, at a given epoch, summarily: 'The artificial or the formal is less worthy than the natural,' without any necessary analysis of what these abstract terms involve. Their æsthetic attention to the concrete case is obstructed by the phrase; and architecture serves as a mere symbol of the idea.

But this, the central point of the Romantic Fallacy, must be guarded from misunderstanding. The influence of literature upon the arts of form exists at all times, and is often beneficial. Romanticism is a permanent force in the mind, to be neither segregated nor expelled. It is only in the manner of its operation that the fallacy occurs. The arts of form have their native standards, their appropriate conventions; standards and conventions founded in experience, and necessary to render them effective in any undertaking, howsoever inspired. When for any reason tradition, which is the vehicle of those standards and conventions, wavers or decays, then the literary influence will, in all likelihood, impose inappropriate standards of its own. The necessary balance between formal and significant elements, which in every art is differently poised, is then overweighted. Overcharged with literary significance and atrophied in its design, the art of form loses the power to impress; it ceases, in any æsthetic sense, to be significant at all.

Thus, in transporting romance from poetry to architecture, it was not considered how different is the position which, in these two arts, the romantic element must occupy. For, in poetry, it is attached *not to the form but to the content*. Coleridge wrote about strange, fantastic, unexpected, or terrible things, but he wrote about them in balanced and conventional metres. He presented his romantic material through a medium that was simple, familiar, and fixed. But in architecture this distinction could not be maintained. When the romantic material entered, the conventional form of necessity disappeared. 'Quaint' design and crooked planning took its place. For here form and content were practically one. And, further, the romantic quality of the material was, in architecture, extremely insecure. The 'magic casements' of Keats have their place in a perfectly formal and conventional metric scheme that displays their beauty, and are powerful over us because they are imagined. But the casements of the romantic architecture, realised in stone, must lack this reticence and this support. They were inconvenient rather than magical, and they opened, not on the 'foam of perilous seas,' but, most often, upon a landscape-garden less faery than forlorn.

Certain images of architecture in their proper context, formal and poetic, are romantic. Remove them from that context, and render them actual, and it becomes evident that there is nothing inherent in the architecture itself that can evoke an imaginative response. Again, there are actual works of architecture that by the lapse of time are almost fused with Nature, and by the course of history almost humanised with life. These, too, are romantic. But if they are repeated anew, it becomes evident that the romantic element was adventitious to the architectural value. The form itself, which must inevitably be the object both of architectural art and criticism, is found to be valueless altogether, or valued only by a vague analogy of thought. And this, in effect, is the case with the conscious architecture of romance. Sharply concrete, divested of the charm of age, it lacks alike the material beauty and the imaginative spell. The formal basis is lacking which alone can give it power.

ɪɪ But the prejudice against the 'unnatural' style of the Renaissance was something more than an association of architecture with *poetical* ideas. As that, indeed, it began. But we shall underrate its force, and falsely analyse its ground, if we do not recognise in it, also, an association of architecture with *ethical* ideas. The poetry of Nature furnished the imagery of the gospel of freedom. The Romantic Movement, with its theory of Natural Rights, gave to Nature a democratic tinge. The cult of Nature had its say on conduct: it was a political creed. It was more; for, in proportion as orthodoxy waned and romanticism gathered force, a worship of Nature—for such, in fact, it was—supplanted the more definite and metaphysical belief. A kind of humility, which once had flowed in fixed, Hebraic channels, found outlet in self-abasement before the majesty, the wildness and the infinite complexity of the physical creation. Of all the changes in feeling which marked the nineteenth century, none perhaps was profounder or more remarkable than this, and none more dramatic in its consequences for art. The instinct of reverence, if science dislodged it from the supernatural world, attached itself to the natural. This sentiment, which for the agnostic mind was a substitute for religion, became for the orthodox also the favourite attitude of its piety. A vague pantheism was common ground between the Anglican Wordsworth, the rationalist Mill, and the revolutionary Shelley. Nature, unadorned, was divine herself—or, at the least, was God's garment and His book; and this, not in the elegant and complimentary sense in which Addison might have so regarded her, but with a profound power to satisfy the mystic's adoration. The argument assumed a different plane. To be 'natural' was no longer a point merely of poetic charm—it was a

point of sanctity. With Ruskin, for example, the argument
from Nature is always final. 'Canst thou draw out Levi-
athan with a hook?' To improve on Nature's architecture
were a like impertinence. It is even suggested that forms
are beautiful precisely in relation to the frequency with
which Nature has employed them. And not only does he
place a sacramental value on the study of Nature deduced
from an arbitrary theological doctrine that it is God's
'book,' but he makes it a sin to study the human instinct,
as though Nature's 'book' had expurgated man, and the
merit of creation ceased at the fifth day. Doubtful logic
this—and scarce orthodox theology! Yet there is little doubt
that Ruskin's reiterated appeal to the example of Nature
to witness against the formal instincts of man, did far more
to enforce the prejudice against the 'foul torrent of the
Renaissance' than he effected either by detailed reasoning
or general abuse. In the face of all this poetry and rhetoric,
in the face of all the sermons that were eloquent in stones,
it is not surprising that Naturalism became the æsthetic
method, and the love of Nature the most genuine emotion
of our age. The emotion was as universal as it was genuine.
A rich harvest of invention rewarded this attentive humility
in the empirical sciences; the generation was encouraged
by Emerson to 'hitch its waggon to a star'; the discipline of
Nature, poetically inspired and religiously sanctioned, was
pragmatically confirmed. Once more in the changes of
civilisation, to 'live according to Nature' became a creed.

But to live according to Nature means also, incidentally, to build and to garden according to Nature. And
since the sublimity of Nature—its claim to worship—lay
in its aloof indifference to man and in its incalculable
variety, to build and garden according to Nature meant, as
the progress of art soon demonstrated, to have a house and
garden which betrayed, so far as possible, no human agency
at all; or, at least, such human agency as might be manifested must be free from one specifically human quality—
the 'self-contemplating reason.' This, with its insistence on

order, symmetry, logic, and proportion, stood, in the ethics of Nature, for the supreme idolatry. [2]

On the one side was Nature: the curves of the waves, the line of the unfolding leaf, the pattern of the crystal. All these might be studied, and in some way architecturally employed—no matter how—so long as the knowledge and the love of them were evident. On the other stood the principles of Palladio, and all the pedantry of rule and measure, made barren by the conscious intellect. The choice between them was a moral choice between reverence and vanity. This was the refrain of *The Stones of Venice* and all the criticism 'according to Nature.'

The cult of Nature has a venerable history; but it is interesting to notice the change it has here undergone. For Nature, as the romantic critics conceive it, is something very different from the Nature which their Stoic predecessors set up as an ideal, and very different also from Nature as it actually is. For the element in Nature which most impressed the Stoics was law, and its throne was the human reason. To 'follow reason' and 'to live according to Nature' for Marcus Aurelius were convertible terms. The human intellect, with its inherent, its 'natural' leanings towards order, balance, and proportion, was a part of Nature, and it was the most admirable and important part. But Nature, in the ethical language of her modern æsthetic devotees, stands most often in definite contradistinction to the human reason. They were willing to recognise authority 'in the round ocean and the living air,' but few remembered with Wordsworth to add: 'and in the mind of man.' The architect's work must be a hymn to creation, must faithfully reflect the typical laws and imitate the specific char-

[2] This may perhaps furnish a philosophic basis for the advice once offered by a French nobleman, when consulted as to the most propitious method of laying out a garden in the then novel Romantic Manner: 'Enivrez le jardinier et suivez dans ses pas.' The 'self-contemplating reason,' temporarily dethroned by this expedient, is, for Ruskin, a constant source of political tyranny, architectural pedantry and spiritual pride.

acter of all that Nature presents. But the typical law and specific character of humanity, to impose order and rhythm on our loose, instinctive movements and proportion on our works—this is the unworthy exercise of 'self-contemplating Greeks,' the mark of 'simpletons and sophists.' While all things in nature fulfil their own law, each after its kind, man alone was to distrust his law and follow that of all the others; and this was called the example of Nature. Yet, since even so some choice is in practice forced upon him, the sole result of 'following Nature' is to sanctify his own caprice. Nature becomes the majestic reminder of human littleness and the insignificance of other people's thought. It is difficult to treat with total seriousness a phase of opinion so fatally paradoxical. Yet it sank deep into the public taste; and even now a discernible taint or moral reproof colours the adverse criticism of formal architecture; and a trace of conscious virtue still attends on crooked planning, quaint design and a preference for Arctic vegetation unsymmetrically disposed.

The creed of Nature entailed two consequences: first, a prejudice against Order and Proportion, and, therefore, against the Renaissance—for however deeply Order and Proportion may characterise the laws of Nature, they are far to seek in its arrangement; secondly, an emphasis on representation, on fidelity to the natural fact. This was soon made apparent in painting—first, in the microscopic realism of the Pre-Raphaelites; later, with more regard to the facts of vision, in impressionism. Architecture—an abstract or, at the least, a utilitarian art—might have been expected to escape. But it contained one element which exposed it to attack: it contained architectural sculpture. It followed, therefore, that this element, which admitted of representation and could be pressed directly into the cult and service of Nature, should become supreme. 'The only admiration worth having,' it is said in *The Seven Lamps*, 'attaches itself wholly to the meaning of the sculpture and the colour of the building.' 'Proportion of masses is mere doggerel.' And not only was sculpture thus thrust out of its true relation and made the chief end and criterion of architecture, but it was required, by the same argument, to be realistic. But architecture, if it means anything, means a supreme control over all the elements of a design, with the right to arrange, to modify, to eliminate and to conventionalise. Here, instead, arrangement becomes 'doggerel' and convention a blasphemy. In this, it will be noticed, the romanticism of Nature reached a conclusion exactly parallel to the romanticism of History. The latter, as we saw, becoming antiquarian, emphasised detail at the expense of the whole, and allowed architectural detail to deteriorate into a stylistic symbol. So, in this case, sculpture takes the place of architecture and deteriorates into realism. All this was necessarily fatal to the Renaissance style. Here there was little sculpture, and that little for the most part was conventional. Artificial in detail, artificial in design, here was an 'unnatural' architecture. Further condemnation could not be required.

III No fashion could have so securely established itself that was rooted in preferences altogether irrational or even new. Naturalism in architecture is partly a poetical taste; partly it is an ethical prejudice, and in each case it has been shown to be fallacious. But naturalism is also frankly æsthetic: a preference not merely of the fancy or the conscience, but of the eye. It may have entered modern architecture by a kind of false analogy, and may still derive from poetry a half-unreal support; but it has a solid footing of its own. For the place of what is unexpected, wild, fantastic, accidental, does not belong to poetry alone. These are the qualities which constitute the *picturesque*—qualities which have always been recognised as possessing a value in the visual arts. And one cause of offence in Renaissance architecture is precisely its lack of this picturesqueness of which Nature is so full. For the sake of this merit to the eye, how much decay has been

endured and awkwardness forgiven! In a theory of architecture, what place then, if any, can be found for this true
merit of the picturesque? What was, in fact, its place in the
architecture of the Renaissance? To these questions an
answer should be given before the romantic criticism of
architecture can be fairly and finally dismissed.

If the wild and the accidental are absent from Renaissance architecture, it is certainly not because the men of
that period were blind to their attraction. The term
pittoresco was, after all, their own invention. It stood, on
its own showing, for the qualities which suggest a picture,
and are of use in the making of it. Picturesque elements—
elements that are curious, fantastic, accidental, had been
sought after in the painting of Italian backgrounds almost
from the first. Their presence gave a special popularity to
such subjects as the Adoration of the Kings, depicted, as
by convention they habitually were, with strange exotic
retinues and every circumstance of the fancied East. Thus
the word itself, when, soon after the middle of the seventeenth century, it came into use, marked not so much a
new virtue in painting as a new analytic interest, taking
note for the first time of a permanent character in the art.
Nor were these romantic elements limited to landscape
and costume. They took the form, often enough, of inventions of fantastic architecture. And this is the more
significant since in the Renaissance painters and architects
are almost one fraternity, and the two arts were frequently
conjoined.

But their sense of the freedom appropriate to the
painted architecture is in strong contrast to the strictness
they imposed upon themselves in the concrete art. The
nearer art approached to the monumental, the more this
self-denying ordinance became severe. Whatever surrounds
us and contains our life; whatever is insistent and dominating; whatever permits us no escape—that, they felt, must
be formal, coherent, and, in some sense, serene. Real architecture, by its very scale and function, is such an art. It
is insistent, dominating, and not to be escaped. The wild,

the fantastic, the unexpected in such an art could not therefore be allowed to capture the design. That, if we may judge from their work, was the principle in which Renaissance architects put faith.

This principle, like all the principles of Renaissance architecture, rested on a psychological fact. The different effects which art is able to produce, however various and incommensurable they may radically be, are commensurable at least in this: that each in some degree makes a demand on our *attention*. Some works of art affect us, as it were, by infiltration, and are calculated to produce an impression that is slow, pervasive, and profound. These seek neither to capture the attention nor to retain it; yet they satisfy it when it is given. Other works arrest us, and by a sharp attack upon the senses or the curiosity, insist on our surrender. Their function is to stimulate and excite. But since, as is well known, we cannot long react to a stimulus of this type, it is essential that the attention should, in these cases, be soon enough released. Otherwise, held captive and provoked, we are confronted with an insistent appeal which, since we can no longer respond to it, must become in time fatiguing or contemptible.

Of these two types of æsthetic appeal, each commands its own dominion; neither is essentially superior to the other, although, since men tend to set a higher value on that which satisfies them longest, it is art of the former kind which has most often been called great. But they do both possess an essential fitness to different occasions. Wherever an occasion either refuses or compels a sustained attention, a right choice between the two types will be a first condition of success. Fantastic architecture, architecture that startles and delights the curiosity and is not dominated by a broad repose, may sometimes be appropriate. On a subdued scale, and hidden in a garden, it may be pleasant enough; but then, to be visited and not lived in. At a theatrical moment it will be right. It may be gay; it may be curious. But it is unfitted, æsthetically, for the normal uses of the art, for it fatigues the attention; and architecture once again is insistent, dominating and not to be escaped.

The practice of the Renaissance was controlled, if not by this reasoned principle, at least by an instinctive sense for its application. Even in the picture—since this, too, must have its measure of attention—the 'picturesque' element is made subordinate; it is subdued to that wider composition of line and tone and colour which contains it. And the complete picture itself is, or should be, subordinate once more to the formal scheme of the architecture, where it fills an appointed place. Consequently, the 'accidental' element, in the final result, is adequately submerged within the formal; it gives, without insistence, the charm of strangeness and variety to a general idea which it is not suffered to confuse.

This the Renaissance allowed; but the Renaissance went further. It was not only in painting that the picturesque could be favourably included; it was not only in its farms and hill-town buildings, pictorial as their beauty is. The Renaissance ended by reconciling the picturesque with classic architecture itself. The two were blended in the Baroque. It is not the least among the paradoxes of that profoundly great style that it possesses, in complete accord, these contrary elements. To give the picturesque its grandest scope, and yet to subdue it to architectural law—this was the baroque experiment and it is achieved. The baroque is not afraid to startle and arrest. Like Nature, it is fantastic, unexpected, varied and grotesque. It is all this in the highest degree. But, unlike Nature, it remains subject rigidly to the laws of scale and composition. It enlarged their scope, but would not modify their stringency. It is not, therefore, in any true sense accidental, irregular, or wild. It makes—for the parallel is exact—a more various use of discords and suspensions, and it stands in a closely similar relation to the simpler and more static style which preceded it, as the later music to the earlier. It enlarged the classic formula by developing within it the principle of movement. But the movement is logical. For baroque ar-

74

chitecture is always[3] logical: it is logical as an æsthetic construction, even where it most neglects the logic of material construction. It insisted on coherent purpose, and its greatest extravagances of design were neither unconsidered nor inconsistent. *It intellectualised the picturesque.*

That the baroque style should be supreme in the garden and in the theatre—the two provinces which permit design its greatest liberty—was to be expected. The fountains and caryatides at Caprarola, the stage conceptions of Bibbiena and Andrea Pozzo, are unsurpassed. But the baroque could satisfy no less the conditions of a monumental and a permanent art. The colonnade of St. Peter's, Bernini's St. Andrea, the Salute at Venice, the front of the Lateran, are 'exciting' architecture: they startle the attention; they have the vivid, pictorial use of light and shade; the stimulus of their effect is sharp. In all this they achieve the immediate merit of the picturesque. Yet their last and permanent impression is of a broad serenity; for they have that baroque assurance which even baroque convulsion cannot rob of its repose. They are fit for permanence; for they have that massive finality of thought which, when we live beside them, we do not question, but accept.

Here, then, in the painting and architecture of the Renaissance, is an example of the fit employment of the picturesque. But these restrictions were not destined to be respected. The cult of Nature, by its necessary hostility to convention, modified that treatment of the picturesque and destroyed in it those saving qualities which can reconcile it with a 'dominating and insistent art': the qualities of reserve, finality, and repose.

While the Renaissance was in its vigour, the romantic

[3] I am speaking throughout of baroque architecture at its best. Naturally, in some cases there is charlatanism, or an ignorant attempt, to imitate the forms without perceiving the theory of the art. But the essence of the modern 'picturesque' taste in architecture is its absence of theory, its insistence on the *casual*.

view of Nature was no enemy of classic architecture. Of
this the painters give us evidence enough. The painting of
Claude Lorrain poeticised Nature in a luminous Virgilian
mood, to which his vision of classic architecture, so far from
being foreign, was the almost necessary complement. Without the austere quiet of his temples, Nature, in its tran-
quillity, might seem less human than he dreamt; without
their Corinthian state, less sumptuous. Poussin, more syl-
van in his interpretation, is not less classic in his forms.
The more dramatic nature-painters—Salvator and the rest
—did not press the wildness of their inspiration beyond
its natural confines. It is perhaps only with Piranesi that a
new spirit begins to show its force. In Piranesi, the greatest
master of the picturesque in art, Nature holds architecture
in its clasp, and, like the 'marble-rooted fig tree,' shatters
and tortures it in its embrace. The consequences which
were in due course to follow from the union are foreshadowed in the earliest phase of this master's art. He
conceived a vision of infernal dungeons, without meaning, exit or hope; architecture, surrendered to the picturesque, was doomed in two generations to fall to the chaos
without achieving the grandeur of Piranesi's 'Carceri.'
Piranesi's etchings were multiplied rapidly and widely cir-
culated; and the effect of their picturesque power on the
imagination of the eighteenth century was decisive. Thus
the way was made ready for the work of literature, and the
new poetry of Nature when it came was reinforced by an
existing fashion. Painting and literature were now as one.
The taste for the picturesque, defensible enough in those
two arts, could not be long constrained within their limits.
A picturesque architecture was required—an architecture
untrammelled by those restraints which even the baroque
style had hitherto observed. The philosophy of the Revolution favoured this impulse of the arts. True, it wrapped
itself at first in a Greek mantle and David contrived a
Doric background for its sages and tyrannicides. But 'natural' rights and a creed of anarchy could not for ever ally
themselves with the most austere, the most conventional

of styles. The philosophy of freedom invoked for architecture, as for life, the magic charm of Nature. But the material of architecture, no less than that of politics, was unfitted to receive its impress. For, in these obdurate forms, variety must prove tedious and licence lose its fascination.

But such an argument is incomplete. Picturesque building, it may be replied, in so far as it is insistent, curious and wilfully capricious, like the modern style of Germany or the fantastic style of the Gothic revival, may be thus unfit. But architecture which aims at the picturesque *need not* be insistent. There is a romanticism of conceits: the romanticism of Chambord, or the poetry of Donne. But there is also a romanticism of natural simplicity: the romanticism of Wordsworth and of a 'rustic' architecture. Architecture, in fact, can be picturesque without affectation, and various without disquiet. Why should not this be favoured? Where is the fault in that domestic type of architecture, in which we see a variety of form conditioned solely by convenience? Here will be repose, because the picturesqueness is unstudied, fitting the house to unselfconscious nature. No insistent appeal is thrust on the attention, for no deliberate appeal exists. This, in our time, is the true rival to the Renaissance style. It is this architecture which has so firm a hold in England, which seems to us so good to paint and good to live in. Poetry and sentiment are in its favour; it indolently provides pleasure to the eye. Leave it to be overgrown and it will be soon 'transformed by the enchantment of Nature to the likeness of her own creations.' Its beauty is secure from fashion, for it is elementary and genuine.

This is true; but how much shall we be willing to forego for the sake of this inoffensive, this sometimes charming, architecture? With what is it contrasted? It is usually implied that the alternative is *mere* formality. Formality, too, has its inherent, its, perhaps equal, charm. But it has more. It is the basis of *design*. Everything in architecture which can hold and interest the intellect; every delight that is complex and sustained; every subtlety of rhythm and grandeur of conception, is built upon formality. Without formality architecture lacks the syntax of its speech. By means of it, architecture attains, as music attains, to a like rank with thought. Formality furnishes its own theme and makes lucid its own argument. 'Formal' architecture is to the 'picturesque' as the whole body of musical art to the lazy hum and vaguely occupying murmur of the summer fields.

All this is sacrificed; and perhaps even that little merit is not gained. Time and decay, colour and the accidents of use, the new perspective from the unforeseen angle of chance vision, may be trusted to give picturesqueness to the austerest architecture. Confusion will not lose its charm because there once was thought. Design is no implacable enemy of the picturesque; but the picturesque *ideal* is at variance with tradition and repugnant to design.

Our concern is here with one point only. It is not, certainly, that the picturesque is without merit; the merit of it is indeed too obvious. It is that, as an ideal, the picturesque renders taste obtuse, or suffers it to remain so. Like a coarse weed, not unbeautiful in itself, it tends to stifle every opportunity of growth. The modern taste for picturesqueness—as the old painters suffice to prove—brought with it nothing that was new. Nature, and man's work, is full of a picturesque beauty that has never passed unnoticed. But the æsthetic content of the picturesque is not constructive and cannot be extended. Nevertheless, it is upon this quality, so low in the scale, so unhopeful for future creation, and so unhelpful for an understanding of the formal past, that modern taste has been concentrated. This is the novelty and the prejudice.

There is a beauty of art and a beauty of Nature. Construction, when it relaxes the principles of design, does not become Nature; it becomes, more probably, slovenly art. Nature, for a living art, is full of suggestion; but it is none the less a resisting force—something to be conquered, modified, adorned. It is only when the force of art is spent, when its attempt is rounded and complete, that Nature, freed from the conflict, stands apart, a separate ideal. It is thus the last sign of an artificial civilisation when Nature takes the place of art. Not without reason, it was the eighteenth century at its close—that great, finished issue and realised pattern—which began the natural cult. For a single moment, while the past still imposed its habit upon thought, disaster was arrested. The cult of Nature was a convention like the rest, and sought a place within the scheme. But the next step was the suicide of taste. Taken in isolation, made hostile to the formal instincts of the mind, Nature led, and can only lead, to chaos; whence issued a monstrous architecture: *informe ingens, cui lumen ademptum.* Thus it was that by the romantic taste the artificial was scorned, though art, whatever else it is, is necessarily that; and it was scorned simply because it was not natural, which no art can hope, by whatever casuistry, to become.

FOUR

The Mechanical Fallacy

Such, in broad outline, were the tendencies, and such, for architecture, the results, of the criticism which drew its inspiration from the Romantic Movement. Very different in its origins, more plausible in its reasoning, but in its issue no less misleading, is the school of theory by which this criticism was succeeded. Not poetry but science, not sentiment but calculation, is now the misguiding influence. It was impossible that the epoch of mechanical invention which followed, with singular exactness, the close of the Renaissance tradition, should be without its effect in fixing the point of view from which that tradition was regarded. The fundamental conceptions of the time were themselves dictated by the scientific investigations for which it became distinguished.

Every activity in life, and even the philosophy of life itself, was interpreted by the method which, in one particular field, had proved so fruitful. Every aspect of things which eluded mechanical explanation became disregarded, or was even forced by violence into mechanical terms. For it was an axiom of scientific method that, only in so far as phenomena could so be rendered, might any profitable results be expected from their study. To this rule the arts proved no exception. But they were affected by the prevailing theories in two contrary directions. In many minds, æsthetics, like all philosophy, became subordinated to the categories of materialistic and mechanical science. On the other hand, those who valued art tended more and more to claim for each art its separate consideration. For, since the essence of the scientific procedure had been the isolation of fields of inquiry—the subjection of each to its own hypothetical treatment—it was natural that the fine arts, also, should withdraw into a sphere of autonomy, and demand exemption from any values but their own. 'Art for art's sake,' for all its ring of æstheticism, was thus, in a sense, a motto typical of the scientific age; and Flaubert, who gave it currency, was an essentially scientific artist. But the fine arts employed their autonomy only to demonstrate their complete subservience to the prevailing scientific preoccupation. Each bowed the knee in a different way. Thus Painting, becoming confessedly impressionistic, concerned itself solely with optical facts, with statements about vision instead of efforts after significance. Literature became realistic, statistical, and documentary. Architecture, founded, as it is, on construction, could be rendered, even more readily than the rest, in the terms of a purely scientific description; its aims, moreover, could easily be converted into the ideals of the engineer. Where mechanical elements indisputably formed the basis, it was natural to pretend that mechanical results were the goal; especially at a time when, in every field of thought, the nature of value was being more or less confused with the means by which it is produced.

Now, although the movement of thought we have just described was in no way allied to the Romantic, and may even, in a measure, be regarded as a reaction against it, yet one characteristic at least the two had in common, and that was an inevitable prejudice against the architecture of the Renaissance. The species of building which the mechanical movement most naturally favoured was the utilitarian—the ingenious bridges, the workshops, the great constructions of triumphant industry, proudly indifferent to form. But, in the 'Battle of the Styles,' as the antithesis between Gothic and Palladian preferences was at that time popularly called, the influences of science reinforced the influences of poetry in giving to the mediæval art a superior prestige. For the Gothic builders were not merely favourites of romance; they had been greatly occupied with the sheer problems of construction. Gothic architecture, strictly speaking, came into existence when the invention of intermittent buttressing had solved the constructive problem which had puzzled the architects of the north ever since they had set out to vault the Roman basilica. The evolution of the Gothic style had been, one might almost say, the predestined progress of that constructive invention. The climax of its effort, and its literal collapse, at Beauvais, was simply the climax and the collapse of a constructive experiment continuously prolonged. In no architecture in the world had so many features shown a more evidently constructive origin, or retained a more constructive purpose, than in the Gothic. The shafts which clustered so richly in the naves were each a necessary and separate articulation in the structural scheme; dividing themselves into the delicate traceries of the roof, construction is still their controlling aim. The Greek style alone could show a constructive basis as defined; and, for a generation interested in mechanical ingenuity, the Gothic had this advantage over the Greek, that its construction was dynamic rather than static, and, by consequence, at once more daring and more intricate. Thus Gothic, remote, fanciful, and mysterious, was, at the same time, exact, calculated, and mechanical: the triumph of science no less than the incarnation of romance. In direct contrast with this stood the architecture of the Renaissance. Here was a style which, as we have seen, had subordinated, deliberately and without hesitation, constructional fact to æsthetic effect. It had not achieved, it seemed not even to have desired, that these two elements should be made to correspond. Where the Renaissance builders wanted the effect of a constructional form, they did not scruple to employ it, even where it no longer fulfilled a constructive purpose. On the other hand, with equal disregard for this kind of truth, those elements of construction which really and effectively supported the fabric, they were constantly at pains to conceal, and even, in concealing, to contradict. Constructive science, which so long had been the mistress of architecture, they treated as her slave; and not content with making mechanical expedients do their work while giving them no outward recognition, they appropriated the forms of a scientific construction to purely decorative uses, and displayed the cornice and pilaster divorced from all practical significance, like a trophy of victory upon their walls. And, in proportion as the Renaissance matured its forms and came to fuller self-consciousness in its methods, this attitude towards construction, which had already been implicit in the architecture of ancient Rome, with its 'irrational' combination of the arch and lintel, became ever more frank, and one might almost say, ever more insolent. Chains and buttresses in concealment did the work which some imposing, but unsound, dome affected to contribute; façades towered into the sky far above the churches, the magnitude of whose interiors they pretended to express, and buildings which, in reality, were composed of several stories, were comprehended within a single classic order.

It is useless to minimise the extent to which such practices were typical of the Renaissance. Although it is only in Italy, and in the seventeenth century, that the most glaring examples are to be found, yet the principles which then reached their climax were latent, and even in many cases visible, from its earliest period. They are inherent in the point of view from which the Renaissance approached the question of æsthetics. And, on the continuous plane of increasing 'insincerity' which the style, as a whole, presents, it would be unreasonable and arbitrary to select this point or that as the limit of justifiable licence, and to decry all that came after, while applauding what went before. This, none the less, is the compromise which is fashionable among those critics who feel that concessions must be made, both to the strictures of the 'Scientific' criticism on the one hand, and to the acknowledged fame of the 'Golden Age' of architecture on the other. But such a procedure is misleading, and evades the real issue. It is, on the contrary, imperative to recognise that the Renaissance claimed and exercised this licence from the first, and to make the closest examination of the doctrines which that claim involves. The relation of construction to design is the fundamental problem of architectural æsthetics, and we should welcome the necessity which the Renaissance style, by raising the question in so acute a form, imposes for its discussion. But the issue is not such a simple one as the 'scientific' criticism invariably assumes.

We must ask, then, what is the true relation of construction to architectural beauty; how did the Renaissance conceive that relation; and how far was it justified in its conception?

Let us begin by attempting, as fairly as we may, to formulate the 'scientific' answer to the first of these questions; let us see where it leads us, and if it leads us into difficulties, let us modify it as best we can, in accordance with the scientific point of view.

'Architecture,' such critics are apt to say, 'architecture *is* construction. Its essential characteristic as an art is that it deals, not with mere patterns of light and shade, but with structural laws. In judging architecture, therefore, this peculiarity, which constitutes its uniqueness as an art, must not be overlooked: on the contrary, since every art is primarily to be judged by its own special qualities, it is precisely by reference to these structural laws that architectural standards must be fixed. That architecture, in short, will be beautiful in which the construction is best, and in which it is most truthfully displayed.' And in support of this contention, the scientific critic will show how, in the Gothic style, every detail confesses a constructive purpose, and delights us by our sense of its fitness for the work which is, just there, precisely required of it. And he will turn to the Doric style and assert the same of that. Both the great styles of the past, he will say, were in fact truthful presentations of a special and perfect constructive principle, the one of the lintel, the other of the vault.

Now, in so far as this argument is based on the Greek and mediæval practice of architecture, it is an argument *a posteriori*. But it is clearly useless to reason dogmatically *a posteriori*, except from the evidence of all the facts. If *all* the architecture which has ever given pleasure confirmed the principle stated in the definition, then the argument would be strong, even if it were not logically conclusive. Admitting, then (for the moment), that the description given of Greek and mediæval architecture is a fair one; admitting, also, the Greek pre-eminence in taste, and the acknowledged beauty of the Gothic, the argument from these is clearly not, in itself, an adequate condemnation of a different practice employed by the Romans and the Renaissance, which has enjoyed its own popularity, and whose case has not yet been tried.

But we may suppose our scientific critic to reply that he does not base his case on authority, but on the merits of his definition: that his argument is, on the contrary, *a priori*, and that he cites Greek and mediæval architecture merely as an illustration. Can we say that the illustration is a fair one? Is it a sufficient description of the Greek and Gothic styles of architecture to say that they are 'good construction, truthfully expressed'? Is it even an accurate description?

Are they, in the first place, 'good construction'? Now, from the purely constructive point of view—the point of view, that is to say, of an engineer—good construction consists in obtaining the necessary results, with complete security and the utmost economy of means. But what are the 'necessary' results? In the case of the Greek and Gothic styles, they are to roof a church or a temple of a certain grandeur and proportion; but the grandeur and proportion were determined not on practical but æsthetic considerations. And what is the greatest economy of means? Certainly not the Doric order, which provides a support immeasurably in excess of what is required. Certainly not the Romanesque, or earliest Gothic, which does the same, and *which delights us for the very reason that it does so.* Greek and mediæval construction, therefore, is not pure construction, but construction for an æsthetic purpose, and it is not, strictly speaking, 'good' construction, for, comstructively, it is often extremely clumsy and wasteful.

Can we now describe it as 'construction truthfully expressed'? Not even this. For the Greek detail, though of constructional origin, is expressive of the devices of building in wood; reproduced in stone, it untruthfully represents the structural facts of the case.

And if by 'truthfully expressed construction' it is meant that the æsthetic *impression* should bring home to us the primary constructive facts (a very favourite *cliché* of our scientific critics), how are we to justify the much applauded 'aspiring' quality of Gothic, its 'soaring' spires and pinnacles? In point of structural fact, every dynamic movement in the edifice is a downward one, seeking the earth; the architect has been at pains to impress us with the idea that every movement is, on the contrary, directed upwards towards the sky. *And we are delighted with the impression.*

And not only does this definition, that the beauty of architecture consists in 'good construction truthfully expressed,' *not* apply to the Greek and mediæval architecture, not only does it contradict qualities of these styles which are so universally enjoyed, but it *does* apply to many an iron railway-station, to a printing press, or to any machine that rightly fulfils its function. Now, although many machines may be beautiful, it would be a *reductio ad absurdum* to be forced to admit that they all are: still more that they are essentially more beautiful than the Greek and Gothic styles of architecture. Yet to this conclusion our definition, as it stands, must lead us.

Clearly, then, when Greek and Gothic buildings are cited in support of the view that the essential virtue of architecture lies in its being 'good construction truthfully expressed,' we must take objection, and say, either these styles, and, *a fortiori*, all others, are essentially bad, or our definition must be amended. The scientific criticism would presumably prefer the latter alternative. Those of its supporters who *identify* architectural beauty with good and truthful construction (and there are many) it must disown; and we may suppose it to modify the definition somewhat as follows:

Beauty, it will say, is necessary to good architecture, and beauty cannot be the same as good construction. But good construction is necessary as well as beauty. We must admit, it will say, that in achieving this necessary combination, some concessions in point of perfect construction must constantly be made. Architecture cannot always be ideally economical in its selection of means to ends, nor perfectly truthful in its statement. And on the other hand, it may happen that the interests of sincere construction may impose some restraint upon the grace or majesty of the design. *But good architecture, nevertheless, must be, on the whole, at once beautiful and constructively sincere.*

But this is to admit that there are two distinct elements— good construction and beauty; that both have value, but are irreducible to terms of one another. How then are we to commensurate these two different elements? If a building have much of the second and little of the first—and this, many will say, is the case of Renaissance architecture —where shall we place it, what value may we put upon it, and how shall we compare it with a building, let us say, where the conditions are reversed and constructive rationality co-exists with only a little modicum of beauty? How is the architect to be guided in the dilemma which will constantly arise, of having to choose between the two? And, imagining an extreme case on either side, how shall we compare a building which charms the eye by its proportions and its elegance, and by the well-disposed light and shade of its projections, but where the intelligence gradually discovers constructive 'irrationality' on every hand, and a building like our supposed railway station, where every physical sense is offended, but which is structurally perfect and sincere? Now, the last question will surely suggest to us that here, at any rate, we are comparing something that is art (though, it may be, faulty art) with something that is not art at all. In other words, that from the point of view of art, the element of beauty is indispensable, while the element of constructive rationality is not. The construction of a building, it might conceivably be suggested, is simply a utilitarian necessity, and exists for art only as a basis or means for creating beauty, somewhat as pigments and canvas exist for the painter. Insecure structures, like fading pigments, are technical faults of art; all other structural considerations are, for the purposes of art, irrelevant. And architectural criticism, in so far as it approaches the subject as an art, ought perhaps to take this view.

But there the scientific criticism should certainly have its reply. Granting, it will say, that beauty is a more essential quality in good architecture than constructive rationality, and that the two elements cannot be identified, and admitting that the criticism of architectural art should accept this point of view, there is still a further consideration. It will claim that architectural beauty, though different from the simple ideal of engineering, is still beauty *of structure*, and, as such, different from pictorial or musical beauty: that it does not reside in patterns of light and shade, or even in the agreeable disposition of masses, but in the structure, in the visible relations of forces. The analogy between construction and the mere material basis of the painter's art, it will say, is false: we take no delight in the way a painter stretches his canvas or compounds his pigments, but we do take delight in the adjustment of support to load, and thrust to thrust. It is no doubt legitimate to add decorative detail to these functional elements; they may be enriched by colour or carving; but our pleasure in the colour and the carving will be pleasure in painting or sculpture; our specifically architectural pleasure will be in the functions of the structural elements themselves. It is in this vivid constructive significance of columns and arches that their architectural beauty lies, and not simply in their colour and shape, as such, and so far as the structural values are absent, and the eye is merely charmed by other qualities, it is no longer architectural beauty that we enjoy. Only, these functional elements must be vividly expressed, and, if necessary, expressed with emphasis and exaggeration. The supporting members must assure us of their support. Thus, the Doric or the Romanesque massiveness, while it was in a sense bad science, was good art; yet its beauty was none the less essentially structural. Thus, the printing press or the railway station will now appropriately fall outside our definition because, although truthfully and perfectly constructed, and fit for their functions, they do not *vividly* enough express what those functions are, nor their fitness for performing them. Structurally perfect, they are still structurally unbeautiful. On the other hand, the arches and pilasters of many Renaissance buildings may be agreeable enough as patterns of form, but are no longer employed for the particular structural purpose for which apparently they are intended, and so, in diminishing the intelligibility and vividness of the whole structure, diminish at the same time its beauty. Thus, the one group fails because, though functional, it is not vivid; the other because, though vivid, it is not functional.

Such, or somewhat such, would be the statement of a 'scientific' view of the relation of construction to architectural design, as we should have it when divested of its more obviously untenable assertions and stated *in extenso*. In the modern criticism of architecture, we are habitually asked to take this view for granted, and the untenable assertions as well; and this is accepted without discussion, purely owing to the mechanical preconceptions of the time, which make all criticisms on the score of 'structure' seem peculiarly convincing. Such a view, even in the modified form in which we have stated it, sets up an ideal of architecture to which indeed the Greek and mediæval builders, on the whole, conformed, but to which the Romans conformed very imperfectly, and to which the Renaissance, in most of its phases, did not conform at all. It cuts us off, as it seems, inevitably, from any sympathy with the latter style. Before accepting this unfortunate conclusion, let us see whether the ideal is as rational and consistent as it sounds.

In the first place, it is clear that the vivid constructive properties of a building, in so far as they are effectively constructive, must exist as *facts*. The security of the building, and hence also of any artistic value it may possess, depends on this; and a support which seemed to be adequate to its load, but actually was not, would, as construction, be wrong. But in so far as they are vivid, they must exist *as appearances*. It is the effect which the constructive properties make on the eye, and not the scientific facts that may be intellectually discoverable about them, which alone can determine their vividness. Construction, it may be granted, is always, or nearly always, in some sense, our concern, but not always in the same sense. The two requirements which architecture so far evidently has are constructive integrity in fact, and constructive vividness in appearance. Now, what our scientific critics have taken for granted, is that because these two requirements have sometimes been satisfied at the same moment, and by the same means, no other way of satisfying them is permissible. But there has been no necessity shown thus far, nor is it easy to imagine one, for insisting that these two qualifications should always be interdependent, and that both must invariably be satisfied at a single stroke. Their value in the building is of a wholly disparate kind: why, then, must they always be achieved by an identical expedient? No doubt when this can be done, it is the simplest and most straightforward way of securing good architectural design. No doubt when we realise that this has been done, there may be a certain intellectual pleasure in the coincidence. But even the Greeks, to whom we are always referred, were far from achieving this coincidence. When they took the primitive Doric construction, and raised it to a perfect æsthetic form, the countless adjustments which they made were all calculated for optical effect. They may not have entailed consequences *contrary* to structural requirements, but at least the optical effect and the structural requirements were distinct. The Renaissance grasped this distinction between the several elements of architectural design with extreme clearness. *It realised that, for certain purposes in architecture, fact counted for everything, and that in certain others, appearance counted for everything. And it took advantage*

of this distinction to the full. It did not insist that the
necessary fact should itself produce the necessary appearance. It considered the questions separately, and was content to secure them by separate means. It no longer had
to dance in fetters. It produced architecture which *looked*
vigorous and stable, and it took adequate measures to see
that it actually *was* so. Let us see what was the alternative.
Greek architecture was simply temple architecture. Here,
architectural art was dealing with a utilitarian problem so
simple that no great inconvenience was encountered in
adjusting its necessary forms to its desired æsthetic character. Nor was there any incongruity between the æsthetic and practical requirements of a Gothic cathedral.
But the moment mediæval building, of which the scientific
criticism thinks so highly, attempted to enlarge its scope, it
was compelled to sacrifice general design to practical convenience, and was thereby usually precluded from securing any æsthetic quality but the picturesque. And even so
it achieved only a very moderate amount of practical convenience. Now the Renaissance architecture had to supply
the utilitarian needs of a still more varied and more fastidious life. Had it remained tied to the ideal of so-called
constructive sincerity, which means no more than an arbitrary insistence that the structural and artistic necessities
of architecture should be satisfied by one and the same
expedient, its search for structural beauty would have been
hampered at every turn. And, since this dilemma was obvious to every one, no one was offended by the means
taken to overcome it.

And not only was the practical range of architecture thus
extended without loss to its æsthetic scope, but that scope
itself was vastly enlarged. In the dome of St. Peter's we see
a construction, the grandeur of which lies precisely in the
self-contained sense of its mass, and the vigorous, powerful
contour which seems to control and support its body. Yet
actually the very attempt to give it this character, to add
this majestically structural effect to the resources of architectural art, meant that Michael Angelo ran counter to the

scientific requirements of a dome. The mass which gives so supreme a sense of power is, in fact, weak. Michael Angelo was forced to rely upon a great chain to hold it in its place, and to this his successors added five great chains more. Had he adhered, as his modern critics would desire, to the Byzantine type of dome, which alone would of itself have been structurally sufficient, he must have crowned St. Peter's with a mass that would have seemed relatively lifeless, meaningless, and inert. Structural 'truth' might have been gained. Structural vividness would have been sacrificed. It was not, therefore, from any disregard of the essential constructive or functional significance of architectural beauty that he so designed the great dome, but, on the contrary, from a determination to secure that beauty and to convey it. It was only from his grasp of the relative place for architecture of constructional fact and constructional appearance, that he was enabled, in so supreme a measure, to succeed. And it was by their sense of the same distinction that the architects of the Renaissance, as a school, not only enriched architecture with new beauty, but were able to dignify the current of ordinary life by bending to its uses the once rigid forms of the antique. And this they did by basing their art frankly on the facts of perception. They appealed, in fact, from abstract logic to psychology.

A similar defence may be entered for the Renaissance practice of combining the arch with the lintel in such a way that the actual structural value of the latter becomes nugatory, and merely valuable as surface decoration, or for its elaborate systems of projections which carry nothing but themselves. If we grant that architectural pleasure is based essentially upon our sympathy with constructive (or, as we have agreed, *apparently* constructive form), then no kind of decoration could be more suitable to architecture than one which, so to say, re-echoes the main theme with which all building is concerned. In Renaissance architecture, one might say, the wall becomes articulate, and expresses its ideal properties through its decoration. A wall is based on one thing, supports another, and forms a transition between the two, and the classic orders, when applied decoratively, represented for the Renaissance builders an ideal expression of these qualities, stated as generalities. The fallacy lies with the scientific prejudice which insists on treating them as particular statements of constructive fact wherever they occur. And, if the Renaissance architects, on their side, sometimes introduced a decorative order where on purely æsthetic considerations the wall would have been better as an undivided surface, or if they introduced a decorative order which was ill-proportioned in itself, or detracted from the spatial qualities of the building—which was, in fact, unsuccessful *as decoration*—this we must view as a fault rather of practice than of theory. And their tendency to abuse their opportunities of pilaster treatment must be held to spring from an excessive zeal for the æsthetics of construction, the nature of which they understood far more exactly and logically than their modern critics, who, while rightly insisting on the fundamental importance of structure not only in architectural science, but in architectural art, overlook the essentially different part which it necessarily plays in these two fields, and who imagine that a knowledge of structural fact must modify, or can modify, our æsthetic reaction to structural appearance.

To this position the scientific criticism would have a last reply. It will answer—(for the complaint has often been made)—that this *apparent* power and vigour of the dome of Michael Angelo depends on the spectator's ignorance of constructive science. In proportion as we realise the hidden forces which such a dome exerts, we must *see* that the dome is raised too high for security, and that the colonnade falls too low to receive the thrust, and that, in any case, the volume of the colonnade is inadequate to the purpose, even were the thrust received.

This is one of the commonest confusions of criticism. Just as, in the previous question, the scientific view fails adequately to distinguish between fact and appearance, so here it fails to mark the relevant distinction between feeling and knowing. Forms impose their own æsthetic character on a duly sensitive attention, quite independently of what we may know, or not know, about them. This is true in regard to scientific knowledge, just as in the last chapter we saw it to be true in reference to historical or literary knowledge. The concavity or convexity of curves, the broad relations of masses, the proportions of part to part, of base to superstructure, of light to shade, speak their own language, and convey their own suggestions of strength or weakness, life or repose. The suggestions of these forms, if they are genuinely felt, will not be modified by anything we may intellectually discover about the complex, mechanical conditions, which in a given situation may actually contradict the apparent message of the forms. The message remains the same. For our capacity to realise the forces at work in a building *intellectually* is, to all intents, unlimited; but our capacity to realise them *æsthetically* is limited. We feel the value of certain curves and certain relations of pressure to resistance by an unconscious (or usually unconscious) analogy with our own movements, our own gestures, our own experiences of weight. By virtue of our subconscious memory of these, we derive our instinctive reactions of pleasure, or the reverse, to such curves and such relations. But the more complex forms of construction can address themselves only to the intelligence, for to these our physical memory supplies no analogies, and is awakened by them to no response. So, too, if there be an exaggerated disparity between the visible bulk of a material and its capacity for resistance, as for instance in the case of steel, it is perfectly easy to make the intellectual calculus of its function in the building, but it is quite impossible to translate it into any terms of our own physical experience. We have no knowledge in ourselves of any such paradoxical relations. Our æsthetic reactions are limited by our power to recreate in ourselves, imaginatively, the physical conditions suggested by the form we see: to transcribe its strength or weakness into terms of our own life. The sweep of the lines of Michael Angelo's dome, the grand sufficiency of its mass, arouse in us, for this reason, a spontaneous delight. The further considerations, so distressing to the mechanical critic, remain, even when we have understood them, on a different plane, unfelt.

This theory of æsthetic must indeed be dealt with more adequately in a later chapter, but even if our scientific assailant refuses to admit the distinction between knowing and feeling to be important, and claims—for to this it seems he is reduced—that æsthetic feeling is consequent on *all* we know, and that architectural beauty lies, in fact, in the intelligibility of structure, his position—and it seems to be the last—is simply met. For if it is to be a case of full understanding, the chains which tie the dome are part of what we understand. Why are we to conjure up the *hidden* forces of the dome, and refuse to think of the chains which counteract them? But, granted the chains, the structure is explained, and the knowledge of the fact should give the scientific critic the satisfaction he desires. And if our pleasure lies in intellectually tracing, not the means by which the structure is made possible, but the relation of the structure to its purpose, then this pleasure would be derivable from the work of the Renaissance architect no less than from that of the mediæval one. For, given that the end proposed by the former is understood to be different—and we have shown that it *was* different—from that proposed by the latter, then the different methods chosen in the two cases are no less exactly adjusted to their ends in the one case than in the other. No doubt when the æsthetic sense is atrophied, when the attention is concentrated upon scientific curiosity, when the Renaissance architect is conceived to have attempted something different from what he did attempt, then the dome of St. Peter's may induce nothing but an intellectual irritation. But then, this attitude to architecture, carried to its logical results, ignores its character as an art altogether, and reduces it simply to engineering; and we have already demonstrated the *reductio ad absurdum* which that involves.

Thus vanishes the argument from structure. The prestige which still, in all our thought, attaches to mechanical considerations, have given to so weak a case a perverse vitality. One central point should, however, be clear from this analysis. It may be restated in conclusion, for it is important. Two senses of 'structure' have been entangled and confused. Structure, in one sense, is the scientific method of 'well-building.' Its aim is *firmness.* Its end is achieved when once the stability of architecture is assured. And any means to that end are, scientifically, justified in proportion to their effectiveness. Structure, but now in a different sense, is also the basis of architectural *'delight.'* For architecture, realised æsthetically, is not mere line or pattern. It is an art in three dimensions, with all the consequence of that. It is an art of spaces and of solids, a felt relation between ponderable things, an adjustment to one another of evident forces, a grouping of material bodies subject *like ourselves* to certain elementary laws. Weight and resistance, burden and effort, weakness and power, are elements in our own experience, and inseparable in that experience from feelings of ease, exultation, or distress. But weight and resistance, weakness and power, are manifest elements also in architecture, which enacts through their means a kind of human drama. Through them the mechanical solutions of mechanical problems achieve an æsthetic interest and an ideal value. Structure, then, is, on the one hand, the technique by which the art of architecture is made possible; and, on the other hand, it is part of its artistic content. But in the first case it is subject to mechanical laws purely, in the second to psychological laws. This double function, or double significance, of structure is the cause of our confusion. For the æsthetic efficacy of structure does not develop or vary *pari passu* with structural technique. They stand in relation to one another, but not in a fixed relation. Some structural expedients, though valid technically, are not valid æsthetically, and *vice versa.* Many forces which operate in the mechanical construction of a building are prominently displayed and sharply realisable. They have a mastery over the imagination far in excess, perhaps, of their effective use. Other forces, of equal moment towards stability, remain hidden from the eye. They escape us altogether; or, calculated by the intellect, still find no echo in our physical imagination. They do not express themselves in our terms. They are not powerful over us for delight.

In proportion as these differences became distinguished, the *art* of architecture was bound to detach itself from mechanical science. The art of architecture studies not structure in itself, but the effect of structure on the human spirit. Empirically, by intuition and example, it learns where to discard, where to conceal, where to emphasise, and where to imitate, the facts of construction. It creates, by degrees, a humanised dynamics. For that task, constructive science is a useful slave, and perhaps a natural ally, but certainly a blind master. The builders of the Renaissance gave architecture for the first time a wholly conscious liberty of aim, and released it from mechanical subservience. To recall the art of architecture to that obedience is to reverse a natural process, and cast away its opportunity. The Mechanical Fallacy, in its zeal for structure, refuses, in the architecture of the Renaissance, an art where structure is raised to the ideal. It looks in poetry for the syntax of a naked prose.

A Note on the Pictures

         Geoffrey Scott's ideas, as put forth in *The Architecture of Humanism*, were profoundly and widely realized in his own time in the United States. The following portfolio of pictures attempts to show some of the variety of the architecture of humanism, first in Europe (which, with an emphasis on Italy, is so much the subject of the book here)—during classical antiquity, and then in the Renaissance, Baroque, and Rococo periods as they swept through Italy, France, Germany, England, and other parts of Europe—and then as adapted so successfully in the United States from 1890 to 1930, or what has justly come to be called the American Renaissance. American classical architecture embraces not only such major monuments as the San Francisco City Hall, the New York Public Library, and Villa Vizcaya in Miami, but also many lesser buildings all over the country. It was a movement so widespread and comprehensive as to include virtually every town and every city neighborhood. The architectural production of this period was enormous and widely varied in style, quality, and complexity, and it constitutes a most important part of the American architectural heritage. Of course, it was in the hands of the master figures such as Arthur Brown, Jr., and McKim, Meade and White—who brought architecture, painting, sculpture, furniture, and interior decorating so grandly and artistically together—that Scott's architecture of humanism was most fully realized in the United States.

—H.S.B.

4. *The Source in Grecian Antiquity*. Façade of the Propylaia, Acropolis, Athens.

5. *The Source in Roman Antiquity*. Detail of the Colosseum, Rome.

6. *The Classical as an Urban Amenity*. Roman Doric order from Bernini's colonnade of St. Peter's, Rome.

7. *The Classical as an Urban Amenity in America*. Detail of the screened colonnade to the New York City Municipal Building, by William Mitchell Kendall of McKim, Mead and White.

8. *Triumphal-Arch Motif in Rococo Germany.* Façade of the pilgrimage church
of Vierzenheiligen, by Johann Balthasar Neumann.

9. *Triumphal-Arch Motif in Grassroots America.* From the Citizens and Southern National Bank, Savannah, Georgia, by Mowbray and Uffinger.

10. *The Architecture of Humanism Comes to the Campus, I.* Garden house at Sweet Briar College, by Cram and Ferguson.

11. *The Architecture of Humanism Comes to the Campus,* II. Colton Chapel, Lafayette College, by Carrière and Hastings.

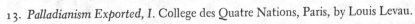

12. *Palladianism Proper.* Palladio's Palazzo Chiericati, Vicenza, Italy.

13. *Palladianism Exported, I.* College des Quatre Nations, Paris, by Louis Levau.

14. *Palladianism Exported*, II. Horse Guards, Whitehall, London, by William Kent and John Vardy.

15. *Palladianism Overseas*. Dallas Hall at Southern Methodist University, Dallas, by Shepley, Rutan, and Coolidge.

16. *The Marriage of Architecture and Sculpture in Italy*. Detail of the Palazzo
Spada, Rome

17. *The Marriage of Architecture and Sculpture in America.* Detail of San Francisco City Hall, by Arthur Brown, Jr.

18. *Classical Details in America, I.* Gilded ceiling from the Interdepartmental Auditorium, Washington, by Arthur Brown, Jr.

19. *Classical Details in America, II.* Lantern from the Interdepartmental Auditorium, Washington, by Arthur Brown, Jr.

20. *Classical Details in a Classical Land*. From the Villa Ludovisi, Rome.

21. *Grand Interior on a Colossal Scale*. From St. John the Lateran Basilica, Rome.

22. *Grand Interior on a Princely Scale*. From the New York Public Library.

23. *The Palace in Italy.* Detail of the Palazzo Farnese, Rome.

24. *The Palace in America*. Detail of the Century Association, New York, by McKim, Mead and White.

25. *The Architectural Use of Painting*. Chamber from the Palazzo della Cancelleria, Rome, with murals by Vasari.

26. *The Architectural Use of Painting in America.* Ceiling by Ezra Winter
from the Cunard Building, New York.

27. *The Architecture of Humanism as a Continuing Tradition*. Detail of the project for the Edward Dinsha house, by John Barrington Bayley.

The Ethical Fallacy

1 'I might insist at length on the absurdity of (Renaissance) construction . . . but it is not the form of this architecture against which I would plead. Its defects are shared by many of the noblest forms of earlier building and might have been entirely atoned for by excellence of spirit. *But it is the moral nature of it which is corrupt.*' [1]

'It is base, unnatural, unfruitful, unenjoyable and impious. Pagan in its origin, proud and unholy in its revival, paralysed in its old age . . . an architecture invented as it seems to make plagiarists of its architects, slaves of its workmen, and sybarites of its inhabitants; an architecture in which intellect is idle, invention impossible, but in which all luxury is gratified and all insolence fortified; the first thing we have to do is to cast it out and shake the dust of it from our feet for ever. Whatever has any connection with the five orders, or with any one of the orders; whatever is Doric or Ionic or Corinthian or Composite, or in any way Grecised or Romanised; whatever betrays the smallest respect for Vitruvian laws or conformity with Palladian work —that we are to endure no more.' [2]

A new temper, it is clear, distinguishes this rhetoric from the criticism we have hitherto considered. The *odium theologicum* has entered in to stimulate the technical controversies of art. The change of temper marks a change, also, in the ground of argument: 'It is the moral nature of it which is corrupt.' Fresh counts are entered in the indict-

[1] *The Stones of Venice*, vol. III. chap. ii. § 4.
[2] *The Stones of Venice*, vol. III. chap. iv. § 35.

ment, while the old charges of dulness or lack of spontaneity, of irrational or unnatural form, are reiterated and upheld before a new tribunal. Barren to the imagination, absurd to the intellect, the poets and professors of construction had declared this architecture to be: it is now repugnant to the conscience and a peril to the soul.

From the confused web of prejudice which invests the appreciation of architecture, we have therefore to disentangle a new group of influences, not indeed always existing separately in criticism, but deriving their persuasive force from a separate motive of assent. The ideals of romanticism and the logic of a mechanical theory are not the sole irrelevancies which falsify our direct perception of architectural form. We see it *ethically*.

How did the ethical judgment come to be accepted as relevant to architectural taste? How far on its own principles did it establish a case against Renaissance architecture? And can those principles find place at all in a rational æsthetic? These are the questions which now require solution, if we are to guard against, or do justice to, a still powerful factor in contemporary taste. For although few serious students of architecture would now confess themselves Ruskinian, and none would endorse those grand anathemas without reserve, the phrases of Ruskin's currency are not extinct. In milder language, certainly, but with even less sense that such ideas require argument or proof, the axioms are reiterated: architecture is still the 'distinctively political' art, its virtue, to 'reflect a national aspiration,' and all the faults and merits of a class or nation are seen reflected in the architecture that serves their use.[3]

[3] It is significant of the now axiomatic character of such ideas that we find them included by courtesy in the works of writers *whose actual bias and method are utterly opposed to the ethical.* Thus Professor Moore, in one of the few volumes which have been devoted to considering Renaissance architecture as a distinctive art, bases his whole treatment quite consistently upon a *mechanical* ideal of architecture: an ideal in which a most scholarly study of Gothic has no doubt con-

The ethical critic of architecture has three different forms of arrow in his quiver, all of which are sent flying at the Renaissance style—an unperturbed Sebastian—in the two passages we have quoted. First, the now blunted shafts of theology: Renaissance architecture is 'impious.' Next, a prick to the social conscience: Renaissance architecture entails conditions, and is demanded by desires that are oppressive and unjust; it 'makes slaves of its workmen and sybarites of its inhabitants.' Last, most poisoned, and the only menace to the martyr's vital part: Renaissance architecture is bad in itself, inherently, because it is insincere (for instance) or ostentatious; because the 'moral nature of it is corrupt.' These darts, if the fury of intolerance

firmed him. Fitness of construction is his sole and invariable test of value. Not one word occurs throughout with regard to any single building about the kind of human character it indicates or promotes. Yet he prefaces this scientific work, not by any declaration of mechanical faith, but by a rapid liturgical recitation of all the ethical formulæ. 'The fine arts,' he says, '*derive their whole character*' from 'the historical antecedents, moral conditions . . . and religious beliefs of the peoples and epochs to which they belong' (the æsthetic sense of a people apparently contributes nothing to the character of their work): 'Into the service of this luxurious and immoral life,' he continues (speaking of the Renaissance), 'the fine arts were now called; and of the motives which animate such a life they become largely the expression.' They 'minister to sensuous pleasure and mundane pride,' and the architect sets himself to his task 'in a corresponding spirit.' The point of interest here is not simply that the principle implied is false or misleading—though it will presently be shown that it is both—but that it is neither demonstrated nor even applied. *It no longer forms part of a conscious system of thought*, but of a general atmosphere of prejudice. The mechanical case derives no authority or support from the ethical case; the ethical case is not illustrated by the mechanical. The ethical formulæ have no function in the argument of the book; they are even opposed to it; but they are so familiar that they can be automatically stated and automatically received. A better example could hardly be desired of that unanalysed confusion in architectural criticism which is the reason of this study.— Charles Moore, *The Character of Renaissance Architecture.*

which first rained them has abated, still stand conspicuous in the body of the saint.

The attack is met on the other side by a contumacious brevity of argument, appropriate indeed to martyrdom, but hardly convincing to the mind. 'The spheres of ethics and æsthetics are totally distinct: ethical criticism is irrelevant to art.' This, together with some manner of diatribe against Ruskin, is all that is vouchsafed in reply when, as now, fashion veers for a moment, and with more ardour than understanding, in the direction of our Georgian manners. 'Ethical criticism is irrelevant to art.' No proposition could well be less obvious. None, we shall see reason to admit, could be less true. But one confusion begets another, and this axiom, too, now adds its darkness to the dim region where the controversies of architecture are sorrowfully conducted.

The ethical case deserves a closer study and a less summary retort.

First, then, for the origins of our habit. The ethical tendency in criticism is consequent upon the two we have already discussed. The Romantic Fallacy paved the way for it. The Mechanical Fallacy provoked it.

The essential fallacy of romanticism was, we saw, that it treated architectural form as primarily symbolic. Now there is evidently no reason why an art of form, if it be regarded as significative at all, should have its meaning limited to an *æsthetic* reference. Romanticism, it is true, was concerned with the imaginative or poetic associations of style. But when once this habit of criticism was established—when once it seemed more natural to attend to what architecture indirectly signified than to what it immediately presented—nothing was required but a slight alteration in the predominant temper of men's minds, an increased urgency of interest outside the field of art, to make them seek in architecture for a *moral* reference. Romanticism had made architecture speak a language not its own—a language that could only communicate to the spectator the thoughts he himself might bring. Architecture had become a mirror to literary preferences and literary distastes. Now, therefore, when the preoccupations inevitable to a time of social change and theological dispute had become predominantly moral, the language of art, reflecting them, was rife with ethical distinctions. The styles of architecture came to symbolise those states of human character in the craftsman, the patron or the public which they could be argued to imply. They were praised or blamed in proportion as those states were morally approved.

But this was something more than romanticism. No doubt, when all the imagery of nature is employed to heighten the contrast between the rugged integrity of the mediæval builders and the servile worldliness of the modern; then, indeed, the ethical criticism is a form of the romantic. The moral appeal becomes imaginative and the religious appeal poetic. Nevertheless, the arguments which could dismiss the Romantic Fallacy will not suffice to meet the ethical case. The difference between the two seems fundamental. It is, as we saw, unreasonable to condemn an architectural purpose because it fails to satisfy a poetic predilection, for the standards of poetry and of architecture are separate in their provinces and equal in their authority. But, *prima facie*, it is not in the same sense unreasonable to condemn an architectural purpose because it offends a moral judgment; for the moral judgment claims an authority superior to the æsthetic, and applies to all purpose and action whatsoever. Hence, architecture falls within its province. If, then, it can be shown that moral values exist at all in architectural style, these, it may be pleaded, must form our ultimate criterion; these will determine what we *ought* to like, and a criticism which ignored their existence would be frivolous and partial. It would not, that is to say, be a final criticism; for to the moral judgment belongs the verdict upon every preference. Why, then, should the criticism of architecture stop short of the last word? And if, from this plain course, the seeming opposition between æsthetic and moral values should deter us, might not æsthetic good

prove, on a due analysis, reducible to terms of moral good?
This reduction, in effect, the ethical criticism of architecture attempted to achieve. Nor was there anything absurd in the attempt.

The ethical criticism, then, though it claims a different sanction and raises a wider issue, arose from the romantic. It arose, also, as a protest against the mechanical theory. Its motive was to assert the human reference of art against the empty cult of abstract technique. We have already seen that the extreme constructional ideal of architecture was no more than a phase of nineteenth century materialism. It ignored feeling. It neglected alike the æsthetic conscience and the moral. It appealed solely to an intellect which recognised no law but the mechanical. It was an episode in the dehumanisation of thought: a process which, carried to its logical conclusion, renders all values unmeaning. Such a process, however powerful its impulse, could not but provoke in many minds an immediate resistance. But it was a resistance in the field of ethics and theology. For here were the interests which materialism seemed most obviously and immediately to challenge: here, at any rate, were the interests which it was all-important to safeguard. Æsthetic values are a luxury; they are readily forgotten when more vital conflicts become acute. Thus, the necessary counter-attack to the movement of science was consequently ethical in temper. Its concern was with conduct and not primarily with art. It was, in effect, a Puritan revival. The intellectual alternative was strict: either a truculent materialism (with consequences for architecture already analysed) or a moralistic ardour more severe than any that had been dominant since the seventeenth century.

Here were two sinister antagonists. The amiable provinces of art, which lay forgotten and unguarded at their side, soon trembled with the conflict. Architecture became a rallying point; for while the constructive basis of the art exposed it obviously to the scientific attack, its ecclesiastical tradition invited for it, no less, a religious defence. In this region, where the air was dense with ancient sentiment, the moral losses suffered in the territory of metaphysics might, even by a shaken army, be made good. It was a Puritan revival, but with this difference: the fervour of Puritanism was now active in vindicating the value of art. It insisted that architecture was something more than a mechanical problem. It gave it a human reference. But, unluckily, this Puritan attack, far from clearing the path of criticism, did but encumber it with fresh confusions no less misleading than the logic of inhuman science. Art was remembered, but the standards of art remained forgotten. The old Puritanism of the seventeenth century had weighed the influence on life of art as a whole. It had condemned it and driven it forth from its Republic with all the firmness, and something less than the courtesy, which Plato extended to the poets. But the Puritanism of the nineteenth century attempted, while retaining art and extolling its dignity, to govern its manifestations. It sought to guide the errant steps of the creative instinct. It sought also to explain its history. And it did so, as was natural to it, by moral laws and divine authority. At Oxford even the Chair of Poetry was disputed between the creeds. And, in architecture, once granted the theological prejudice, æsthetic dogmas are not likely to be lacking to prove that all the vices which were supposed to have accompanied the return of the Roman style in Europe must be inherent also in the Roman architecture itself. These dogmas survive the sectarian quarrel which gave them birth. The charge outlives its motive; and Renaissance architecture is still for many a critic the architecture of ostentation and insincerity once attributed to a 'Jesuit' art.

The sectarian import of style, though somewhat capriciously determined, might provide an amusing study. The Roman architecture stood for the Church of Rome. The association was natural, and had not the Papacy identified itself with the Renaissance almost at the same time and in the same spirit as it had provoked the rise of Protestantism? Thus the classical forms, although a generation earlier they had echoed in many a Georgian church to strictly Evangelical admonitions, were now arbitrarily associated with the Pope, or—should their severity be in any way mitigated —with the Jesuits. The Gothic, on the other hand—Pugin notwithstanding—was commonly regarded as the pledge of a Protestant or, at the worst, of an unworldly faith. And it is easy to understand that in the days of Bradlaugh and of Newman, these rectitudes of architectural doctrine were of greater moment than æsthetic laws.

The soil was therefore prepared. The sects had ploughed upon it their insistent furrows. And now the winds of architectural doctrine blew loudly, bearing strange seed. The harvest which resulted is historic. *The Seven Lamps* appeared and *The Stones of Venice*. The method of the new criticism was impressive and amazing. For here, side by side with plans and sections, mouldings, and all the circumstance of technical detail, the purposes of the universe were clearly, and perhaps accurately, set forth, with a profusion as generous as, in this subject, it had previously been rare. The prophets Samuel and Jeremiah usurp the authority of Vitruvius. They certainly exceed his rigour. Dangers no less desperate than unexpected are seen to attend the carving of a capital or the building of a door; and the destruction of Gomorrah is frequently recalled to indicate the just, if not the probable, consequences of an error in these undertakings.

But the new criticism did not limit itself to denunciation. A moral code, at once eloquent and exact, was furnished for the architect's guidance and defence, and determined the 'universal and easily applicable law of right' for buttress and capital, aperture, archline and shaft. An immense store of learning and research, of reason also, and sensitive analysis, far superior to that which Ruskin brought to painting, lay imbedded in these splendid admonitions, and seemed to confirm the moral thesis. And it no doubt added greatly to the plausibility of the case that the principles which he presented with the thunder and pageantry of an Apocalypse had been carried out, from foundation to cornice, in almost meticulous detail. Impressive principles of right! They could be fitted to every case, and as we read we cannot but suspect that they are able to establish any conclusion.

The moralistic criticism of the arts is more ancient, more profound, and might be more convincing, than the particular expression which Ruskin gave to it. It is not specifically Christian. It dominates the fourth book of Plato's *Republic* no less than the gospel of Savonarola. It is one of the recurrent phases of men's thought: a latent tendency which it was Ruskin's mission rather to re-awaken than create. The ethical criticism of architecture is likely therefore to survive the decay of the individual influence which brought it back to force. The dictator's authority has long since, by his own extravagance, been destroyed. The casuistries of *The Stones of Venice* are forgotten; its inconsistencies quite irrelevant to the case. They are the unchecked perversities of genius, which an ethical criticism is not bound to defend, and which it would be idle, therefore, to attack. We are concerned, not with the eccentricities of the leader, but with the possible value and permanent danger of the movement which he led. And it is more necessary at this date to emphasise the service which he rendered than to decry the logic of his onslaught.

In the first place, Ruskin undoubtedly raised the dignity of his subject, no less than he widened its appeal. He made architecture seem important, as no other critic had succeeded in doing. The sound and the fury, not unduly charged with significance; the colour of his periods; the eloquence which casts suspicion on the soundest argument and reconciles us to the weakest; the flaming prophecies and the passionate unreason, had that effect at least. They were intensely dynamic.

In the second place, it is fair to remember that Ruskin asserted the *psychological* reference of architecture. No ingenuity of technique would satisfy him, nor any abstract accuracy of scholarship, however mediæval. Mere legalism, mere mechanism, mere convention, and everything which, outside the spirit of man, might exercise lordship over the arts he combated. No doubt his psychology was false. No doubt he utterly misinterpreted the motive of the craftsman and dogmatised too easily on the feelings of the spectator. Probably he took too slight account of the love of beauty as an emotion independent of our other desires. But still in some sense, however illusory, and by some semblance of method, however capricious, the principle was maintained: that the arts must be justified by the way they make men feel; and that, apart from this, no canon of forms, academic, archæological or scientific, could claim any authority whatsoever over taste. This was a great advance upon the mechanical criticism; it was an advance, in principle, upon the hieratic teaching of the schools.

But the psychological basis which Ruskin sought to establish for architecture was exclusively moral, and it was moral in the narrowest sense. He searched the Scriptures; and although the opinion of the prophets on Vitruvian building might seem to be more eloquent than precise, he succeeded in enlisting in favour of his prejudices an amazing body of inspired support. But it is easy to see that an equal expenditure of ingenuity might have produced as many oracles in defence of Palladio as it showed grounds for his perdition. The time is gone by when scholars, passing to their innocent tasks through the courts of Hawkesmoor or of Wren, were startled to recognise the Abomination of Desolation standing, previously unnoticed, in the place where it ought not. And a criticism which would be willing—were they propitious—to prove a point of theory by citing the measurements of the Ark, must now seem obsolete enough. But if the theological argument has ceased to be effective, its interest for the history of taste remains immense. And the fact that, a hundred years after Voltaire, one of the foremost men of letters in Europe should have looked for architectural guidance in the Book of Lamentations is one which may well continue to delight the curiosity of anthropologists when the problems of æsthetic have been rejected as unfruitful, or abandoned as solved.

II   More persuasive than the theological
prejudice, and more permanent, is the political. If, as we
have said, the romantic fallacy reduced taste to a mere
echo of contemporary idealism, if it encouraged men to
look in art always for a reflection of their existing dreams,
what must be the verdict on Renaissance architecture of
an age whose idealism was political and whose political
ideal was democracy? For here was an architecture rooted
in aristocracy, dependent on the very organisation against
which society was now reacting. It had grown up along
with the abuses which were henceforth to be expelled from
the moral ordering of life. And these abuses—to use the
question-begging phrase of modern criticism—'it expressed.'[4] It had exalted princes and ministered to popes.
It stood for the subordination of the detail to the design,
of the craftsman to the architect, of conscience to authority, of whim to civilisation, of the individual will to an
organised control. These things were hateful to the philosophy of revolution. They were hateful no less to the
philosophy of *laissez faire*. The architecture of the Renaissance shared inevitably their condemnation. Moreover, the
minds alike of the good citizen who gloried in industrial-
ism, and of the thinker who shrank from it, were turned
to the future rather than the past. Even the mediæval day-
dreams of Morris were a propaganda and essentially
prophetic. Now the neo-Gothic experiment and the architecture of steel, whatever their initial failures, could
claim to be still untried; from them might still spring the

[4] Abuses in the organisation of society may sometimes, as
in the French eighteenth century, be a precondition of certain
achievements in the arts. But the artistic achievements do not
on that account 'express' the social conditions, though the one
may recall the other to our mind. It would be as true to say
that the view from a mountain 'expressed' the fatigue of get-
ting to the top. Whether the mountain is worth climbing is
another question.

undreamt-of pinnacles which should crown the Utopias of the capitalist and the reformer. But the Renaissance style represented inertia, and the hypocrisy of a dead convention. It promised nothing, and in the commercial monotony of the time the joy that had been in it had died out. 'The base Renaissance architects of Venice,' remarks Ruskin bitterly, 'liked masquing and fiddling, so they covered their work with comic masks and musical instruments. Even that was better than our English way of liking nothing and professing to like triglyphs.' [5] A gloomy style, then; a veritable Bastille of oppressive memories; a style to be cast down and the dust of it shaken 'from our feet for ever.'

On its constructive side the new criticism was no less flattering to a democratic sentiment. It set out to establish, and delighted its public by providing, a 'universal and conclusive law of right' that should be 'easily applicable to all possible architectural inventions of the human mind'; and this in the 'full belief' that in these matters *men are intended without excessive difficulty* to know good things from bad.' Good and bad, in fact, were to be as gaily distinguishable in architecture as they notoriously are in conduct. And the same criterion should do service for both. Because a knowledge of the Orders, which was the basis of architectural training, is not, of itself, a passport either to architectural taste or practice, it was argued that training as such was corrupting. The exactitudes of taste, the trained and organised discrimination which, in the collapse of the old order, men had indubitably lost, were declared to be of less service in framing a right judgment of architecture than the moral delicacy they conceived themselves to have acquired. From the fact that the sculptures of a village church have, or once had, an intelligible interest for the peasant, it is argued that all architecture should address itself to the level of his understanding; and this paradox is so garnished with noble phrases that we have well-nigh

[5] *The Stones of Venice,* vol. i. chap. ii. p. 13.

come to overlook its eccentricity. This prejudice against a trained discernment is significantly universal among writers of the ethical school. They describe it as 'pride,' as 'pedantry,' as 'affection';[6] a habit of speech which would be inexplicable since, after all, training is not a very obvious vice or fatal disqualification, did we not relate it to the combination of romanticism and democracy in which this view of architecture takes its rise. But their habit makes it easy to understand that the ethical criticism was certain to gain ground. It appealed to a sincere desire for beauty in a society that had cast off, along with the traditions of the past, the means by which a general grasp of architectural beauty had in fact been maintained. It offered the privileges of culture without demanding its patience. A new public had been called into being. Works on architecture could never again be addressed: 'To all Joiners, Masons, Plasterers, etc., and their Noble Patrons.' A vast democracy was henceforth to exercise its veto upon taste. Ruskin was the first to capture its attention for the art of building, and it was natural that a public which he had enfranchised should accept from him its creed. It had no effective experience either in the creation or in the patronage of architecture by which that creed might be corrected. Architecture supposedly 'Ruskinian'—though not always to the master's taste—triumphed henceforth in every competition. Architecture in modern theory was a book for all to read. Democracy, looking to the memorials of a world it had destroyed for some image of its own desires, saw in the writing on the wall a propitious index of its own destiny. The orders of Palladio which had dignified the palaces of the *ancien régime* were easily deciphered: Mene, Mene, Tekel, Upharsin. Thus the history of architecture was made a pledge of social justice, and the political currents, strongly running, destroyed all understanding of the Renaissance.

The political prejudice in taste justifies itself by an appeal to moral values; but it does not, like the theological prejudice, indulge in oracles from revelation. It is ethical,

[6] e.g. *The Stones of Venice*, vol. iii. chap. ii. § 38.

but it is ethical in a utilitarian sense. It judges the styles of architecture, not intrinsically, but by their supposed effects. The critic is sometimes thinking of the consequences of a work upon the craftsman; sometimes of the ends which the work is set to serve, and of its consequences upon the public. But in all cases his mind moves straight to the attendant conditions and ultimate results of building in one way rather than another. The importance of the matter is a social importance; the life of society is thought of as an essentially indivisible whole, and that fragment of it which is the life of architecture cannot—it is suggested—be really good, if it is good at the expense of society; and to a properly sensitive conscience it cannot even be agreeable. Purchased at that price, it becomes, in every sense, or in the most important sense, bad architecture. The architectural doctrines of such a man as Morris—a picturesque fusion of artistic with democratic propaganda—are for the most part of this type. The underlying argument is simple. Ethics—or politics—claim, of necessity, precisely the same control over æsthetic value that architecture, in its turn, exercises by right over the subordinate functions of sculpture and the minor arts; and Renaissance architecture is rejected from their scheme.

Even so, it is clear that criticism will still have two factors to consider: the æsthetic quality of architecture and its social result. To confuse the social consequences with the æsthetic value would be an ordinary instance of the Romantic Fallacy. Those were not necessarily the worst poets whom Plato urbanely ushered out of his Republic; for the practical results of an art are distinct from its essential quality. Even for our practice we require a theory of æsthetic value as well as a theory of ethical value, if only in order to give it its place within the ethical scheme. The order of thought should be: what are the æsthetic merits of a style; what is their social value; how far are these outweighed by their attendant social disadvantages?

But the critics of architecture who assail the Renaissance style are far from proceeding in this sequence; nor do they

establish their social facts. We may well doubt whether the
inspired Gothic craftsman of that socialist Utopia ever existed in the Middle Ages. No historical proof of his existence is advanced. If we base our judgment on the
Chronicle of Fra Salimbene rather than on the Dream of
John Ball, which has the disadvantage of having been
dreamt five hundred years later, we shall conclude that the
Gothic craftsman was more probably a man not unlike his
successors, who over-estimated his own skill, grumbled at
his wages, and took things, on the whole, as they came.
Some stress is not untruly laid upon his 'liberty'; a Gothic
capital was, now and then, left to his individual imagination. But how minute, after all, is this element in the whole
picture. The stress laid upon its springs from that disproportionate interest in *sculpture* as opposed to architecture,
the causes of which have already been traced to Romanticism and the cult of Nature. But just as sculpture is not
the æsthetic end of architecture, so, too, sculpture is but a
small part of its practical concern. The foundations are to
be laid, the walls and piers erected, the arches and the
vaultings set. In all this labour there was nothing to choose
between the Mediæval and the Renaissance style: neither
more nor less liberty, neither more nor less joy in the work.
The Renaissance, too, had its painting and its minor arts
—its goldsmiths, carvers and embroiderers—destined in due
course to enrich what had been built. Here, if we trust
the pages of Vasari and Cellini, was no lack of life and
individual stir.

The Renaissance 'slave' toiling at his ungrateful and mechanical task is, no less, a myth. Such persons as may have
formed any intimacy with his successor, the Italian mason,
on his native ground, will realise that he is capable of taking
as vital a pride and as lively a satisfaction in the carving of
his Ionic capital as the mediæval worker may be supposed
to have derived from the manufacture of a gargoyle; that
he by no means repeats himself in servile iteration but
finds means to render the products of his labour '*tutti
variati*'; and that so far from slavishly surrendering to the

superior will of his architect, he permits himself the widest liberty *perchè crede di far meglio*,—whereby, indeed, now as in the past, many excellent designs have been frustrated.

But the mediæval labourer, in this Elysian picture, has his toil lightened by religious aspiration. No doubt he took pleasure in his cult and got comfort from his gods. But how was it with the Renaissance workman at the lowest point of his 'slavery and degradation,' the dull tool whose soulless life is revealed in the baroque? This is Ranke's description of the raising of the great obelisk before the front of St. Peter's, which Domenico Fontana undertook for Sixtus v.:—

'It was a work of the utmost difficulty—to raise it from its base near the sacristy of the old church of St. Peter, to remove it entire, and to fix it on a new site. All engaged in it seemed inspired with the feeling that they were undertaking a work which would be renowned through all the ages. The workmen, nine hundred in number, began by hearing Mass, confessing, and receiving the Communion. They then entered the space which had been marked out for the scene of their labours by a fence or railing. The master placed himself on an elevated seat. The obelisk was covered with matting and boards, bound round it with strong iron hoops; thirty-five windlasses were to set in motion the monstrous machine which was to raise it with strong ropes; each windlass was worked by two horses and ten men. At length a trumpet gave the signal. The very first turn took excellent effect; the obelisk was heaved from the base on which it had rested for fifteen hundred years; at the twelfth, it was raised two palms and a quarter, and remained steady; the master saw the huge mass, weighing, with its casings, above a million of Roman pounds, in his power. It was carefully noted that this took place on the 30th April 1586, about the twentieth hour (about three in the afternoon). A signal was fired from Fort St. Angelo, all the bells in the city rang, and the workmen carried their master in triumph around the inclosure, with incessant shouts and acclamations.

'Seven days afterwards the obelisk was let down in the same skilful manner, upon rollers, on which it was then conveyed to its new destination. It was not till after the termination of the hot months that they ventured to proceed to its re-erection.

'The Pope chose for this undertaking the 10th of September, a Wednesday, which he had always found to be a fortunate day, and the last before the feast of the Elevation of the Cross, to which the obelisk was to be dedicated. On this occasion, as before, the workmen began by recommending themselves to God; they fell on their knees as soon as they entered the inclosure. Fontana had not omitted to profit by the suggestions contained in a description by Ammianus Marcellinus of the last raising of an obelisk, and had likewise provided the power of one hundred and forty horses. It was esteemed a peculiar good fortune that the sky was covered on that day. Everything went well: the obelisk was moved by three great efforts, and an hour before sunset it sank upon its pedestal on the backs of the four bronze lions which appear to support it. The exultation of the people was indescribable and the satisfaction of the Pope complete. He remarked in his diary that he had succeeded in the most difficult enterprise which the mind of man could imagine. He caused medals commemorating it to be struck, received congratulatory poems in every language, and sent formal announcements of it to all potentates. He affixed a strange inscription, boasting that he had wrested this monument from the emperors Augustus and Tiberius, and consecrated it to the Holy Cross; in sign of which he caused a cross to be placed upon it, in which was inclosed a supposed piece of the true Cross.' [7]

[7] Ranke's *History of the Popes*, trans. S. Austin, vol. 1. book iv. § 8. I have quoted the passage at length because, besides indicating the religious enthusiasm of the workmen, and their delight in the work (two supposed monopolies of the Gothic builders), it illustrates the superb spirit of the baroque Pope, who gave Rome, for the second time, an imperial architecture.

The modern labourer has lost these joys; but he has not lost them on account of his Palladian occupations. Whether he be set to build the Foreign Office in the Italian manner, or the Law Courts in the mediæval manner, or a model settlement in the democratic manner, his pagan pleasure and his piety are equally to seek. Here, indeed, is the fallacy of the writers of this school: an idealised mediævalism is contrasted with a sharply realistic picture of Renaissance architecture in modern life: the historical Renaissance, the historical Gothic, they are at no pains to reconstruct. Conducted without impartiality, arguments such as these are but the romance of criticism; they can intensify and decorate our prejudices, but cannot render them convincing. Even so, and did they prove their case, the superior worth of a society might justify the choice, but would not prove the merit of the style of architecture which that society imposed. The æsthetic value of style would still remain to be discussed. Or is that, too, upon a due analysis, within the province of an ethical perception? That is the question which still remains.

III The last phase of ethical criticism has at least this merit, that it strikes at architecture, not its setting. It takes the kernel from its shell before pronouncing upon taste.

There are those who claim a *direct* perception in architectural forms of moral flavours. They say, for example, of the baroque (for although such hostile judgments are passed upon the whole Renaissance, it is the seventeenth century style which most often and most acutely provokes them) that it is slovenly, ostentatious, and false. And nothing, they insist, but a bluntness of perception in regard to these qualities, nothing, consequently, but a moral insensibility, can enable us to accept it, being this, in place of an architecture which should be—as architecture can be—patiently finished and true. Baroque conceptions bear with

them their own proof that they sprang from a diseased
character; and his character must be equally diseased who
can at any subsequent time take pleasure in them or think
them beautiful. They may have grown up in a corrupt society and served ignoble uses. That fact would but confirm
our judgment: it does not furnish its ground. Its ground
is in the work itself; and this is not bad because it is ugly;
it is ugly because, being false, ostentatious, slovenly and
gross, it is obviously and literally bad.

This contention is supported by admitted facts. The detail of the baroque style is rough. It is not finished with
the loving care of the *quattrocento,* or even of the somewhat clumsy Gothic. It often makes no effort to represent
anything in particular, or even to commit itself to any
definite form. It makes shift with tumbled draperies which
have no serious relation to the human structure; it delights
in vague volutes that have no serious relation to the architectural structure. It is rapid and inexact. It reveals, therefore, a slovenly character and can only please a slovenly
attention.

The facts are true, but the deduction is false. If the baroque builders had wished to save themselves trouble it
would have been easy to refrain from decoration altogether, and acquire, it may be, moral approbation for 'severity.' But they had a definite purpose in view, and the
purpose was exact, though it required 'inexact' architecture
for its fulfilment. They wished to communicate, through
architecture, a sense of exultant vigour and overflowing
strength. So far, presumably, their purpose was not ignoble.
An unequalled knowledge of the æsthetics of architecture
determined the means which they adopted. First, for
strength, the building must be realised *as a mass,* a thing
welded together, not parcelled, distributed and joined.
Hence, the composition (the æsthetic unity of parts) must
be imposing; and no one has yet suggested that the baroque architects lacked composition—either the zeal for it
or the power. Next, again for the effect of mass, the parts
should appear to flow together, merge into one another,

spring from one another, and form, as it were, a fused gigantic organism through which currents of continuous vigour might be conceived to run. A lack of individual distinctness in the parts—a lack of the intellectual differentiation which Bramante, for example, might have given them—was thus not a negative neglect, but a positive demand. Their 'inexactness' was a necessary invention. Further—again for the suggestion of strength—the *scale* should be large; and hence, since a rough texture maintains a larger scale than a smooth, an inexact finish was preferred to one more perfect. Last, for the quality of exultation: for vigour not latent but in action; for vigour, so to speak, at play. To communicate this the baroque architects conceived of Movement, tossing and returning; movement unrestrained, yet not destructive of that essential repose which comes from composition, nor exhaustive of that reserve of energy implied in masses, when, as here, they are truly and significantly massed. But since the architecture itself does not move, and the movement is in our attention, drawn here and there by the design, held and liberated by its stress and accent, everything must depend upon the kind of attention the design invites. An attention that is restrained, however worthily, at the several points of the design; an attention at close focus and supplied by what it sees with a satisfying interest; an attention which is not *led on*, would yield no paramount sense of movement. Strength there might be, but not *overflowing* strength; there would be no sense of strength 'at play.' For this reason there exist in baroque architecture rhythm and direction and stress, but no repose—discord, even—till the eye comes to rest in the broad unity of the scheme, and the movements of the attention are resolved on its controlling lines. In proportion as the movement is tempestuous, these lines are emphatic; in proportion as it is bold, these are strong. Hence, sometimes, the necessity—a necessity of æsthetic, if not of constructive logic—for that worst insolence and outrage upon academic taste, the triple pediment with its thrice-repeated lines, placed, like the chords in the last bars of a symphony, to close the tumult and to restore the eye its calm.

In this sense alone is baroque architecture—in the hands of its greatest masters—slovenly or ostentatious, and for these reasons. But we do not complain of a cataract that it is slovenly, nor find ostentation in the shout of an army. The moral judgment of the critic was here unsound because the purpose of the architect was misconceived; and that was attributed to coarseness of character which was, in fact, a fine penetration of the mind. The methods of the baroque, granted its end, are justified. Other architectures, by other means, have conveyed strength in repose. These styles may be yet grander, and of an interest more satisfying and profound. But the laughter of strength is expressed in one style only: the Italian baroque architecture of the seventeenth century.

This brings us to the last charge. Real strength, the critic can reply, may be suffered to be exultant, though it is nobler in restraint. But the strength of the baroque is a deceit. It 'protests too much,' and for the usual reason: that its boast is insecure. Its mass is all too probably less huge, its vistas less prolonged, its richness less precious, than it pretends. The charge of false construction, as construction, has, it is true, been dealt with; the argument from science fell, as we saw, to nothing. But this is an argument of moral taste. Can we approve a style thus saturated with deceit: a style of false façades, false perspectives, false masonry and false gold? For all these, it must be agreed, are found in the baroque as they are found in no other style of architecture. It is an art, not indeed always, but far too often, of 'deceit.'

This is probably the commonest of all the prejudices against the Renaissance style in its full development. But here, too, the facts are sounder than the conclusions.

The harmfulness of deceit lies, it must be supposed, either as a quality in the will of the deceiver, or in the damage inflicted by the deceit. If, in discharge of a debt, a man were to give me instead of a sovereign a gilded farthing, he would fail, no doubt, of his promise, which was to give me the value of twenty shillings. To deceive me was essential to his plan and the desire to do so implied in his attempt. But if, when I have lent him nothing, he were to give me a gilt farthing because I wanted something bright, and because he could not afford the sovereign and must give me the bright farthing or nothing bright at all, then, though the coin might be a false sovereign, there is evidently neither evil will nor injury. There is no failure of promise because no promise has been made. There is a false coin which, incidentally, may 'deceive' me; but there is no damage and no implied determination to deceive, because what I required in this case was not a sovereign but the visible effect of a sovereign, and that he proposed to give—and gave.[8]

I am probably *not* persuaded into believing that the false window of a Renaissance front is a real one, and the more familiar I am with Renaissance architecture, the less likely am I to believe it; but neither do I wish to believe

[8] This may seem obvious enough, and too obvious; but, as Wordsworth wrote in a famous preface: 'If it shall appear to some that my labour is unnecessary and that I am like a man fighting a battle without enemies, such persons may be reminded that whatever be the language outwardly holden by men, a practical faith in the opinion which I am wishing to establish is almost unknown. If my conclusions be admitted, and carried as far as they must be carried if admitted at all, our judgments . . . will be far different from what they are at present, both when we praise and when we censure.' It is, in fact, for lack of stating the case at length and rendering it obvious, that the attack on the inherent falsity of the baroque is repeated in every history of architecture which appears in this country or in France. The attack varies in severity, and in extent. Either the whole Renaissance style is made 'intolerable' by deceit, or it becomes intolerable at its seventeenth century climax; or, if not intolerable, it is a very serious blemish and to be apologised for. But no critic desires or, desiring, has the courage to justify the Renaissance method, *qua* method, root and branch, and to insist that the baroque style was the first to grasp the psychological basis, and consequent liberties of architectural art. Yet such is the fact.

it, nor does it matter to me if, by chance, I am persuaded. I want the window for the sake of the balance which it can give to the design. If the window, in regard to its utilitarian properties, had been wanted at that point, presumably it would have been made. But, on the contrary, it was —very likely—definitely *not* wanted. But its æsthetic properties—a patch of its colour, shape and position—*were* required in the design, and these I have been given. Had it been otherwise there would have been artistic disappointment; as it is, there is no disappointment either practical or artistic. And there is no deceit, for, as the architect is aware, the facts, should I choose to know them, are readily discoverable. True, if I find the apparent stonework of the window is false, there is an element of genuine æsthetic disappointment, for the quality of the material has its own æsthetic beauty. But the baroque architects did not prefer paint to stone. Ruskin was not more disappointed than Palladio that the palaces of Vicenza are of stucco. Few generations realised more clearly the æsthetic quality of rich material; as the bronze and *lapis lazuli* of the altar of S. Ignazio in the Roman *Gesù* may suffice to show. But these architects placed æsthetic values in the scale of their importance, and where economic or other barriers stood in their way, preferred at least, and foremost, to indicate *design*. And, since, in the rich material, part only of the charm resides in the imaginative value of its preciousness—its rarity, the distance it has come, the labours and sacrifices it has cost—and a far greater part in the material beauty, for the sake of which those sacrifices are made, those labours undertaken, the baroque architects, seeing this, sought to secure the last by brilliant imitation, even when, of necessity, they forewent the first. Nor was the imitation, like many that are modern, sordid and commercial—a meticulous forgery. It was a brave impressionism, fit to satisfy the eye. The mind was deluded, if at all, then merrily, and for a moment.

An impartial spectator who found so much contrived— and so ingenuously—for his delight would, on taking thought, no more complain of all these substitutions—these false perspectives and painted shadows—than grow indignant because, in the Greek cornice, he is shown false eggs and darts. For this is no mere flippancy. Imitation runs through art; and Plato was more logical who rejected art, on this account, altogether, than are those critics who draw a line at the baroque. When we have imitated in one way long enough, our convention is accepted as such. The egg and dart moulding is a convention. The baroque habit is a convention also. It is objected that it is a convention which actually deceives and disappoints. But when we are familiar with it, and have ceased desiring to be shocked, this is no longer the case. Its critics, in fact, complain of the baroque that in it they encounter deceit too often; the cause of the complaint is that they have not encountered it enough.

Morally, then, Renaissance 'deceit' is justified. It does not follow on that account that *æsthetically* it is always equally to be admitted. If 'deceit' is carried beyond a certain point, we cease to get architecture and find stage decoration. There is nothing wrong about stage decoration; in its place there is not even anything æsthetically undesirable. It has a sole defect: that it fails—and must fail inevitably—to give us a high sense of permanence and strength. But these are qualities which are appropriate, above all others, in a monumental art; qualities, therefore, which we have a right to expect in architecture. Here, then, is some justification for the theory that the *degree* of pretence is important. True, it is important æsthetically, and not morally, but it is important. But then the baroque style had the most penetrating sense of this importance. It recognised that the liberty to pretend—which the Renaissance had claimed from the beginning—though unlimited in principle, must be subject in practice to the conditions of each particular problem that the architect might undertake. It was a question of psychology. The scope of architecture, in a period as keenly creative as the seventeenth century, was a wide one; its influence was felt through everything that was made. The gaiety of life, no less than its solemn permanency, sought architectural expression. And the baroque style—the pre-eminent style of the pleasure-house, of the garden—was able to minister to this gaiety. The æsthetic pleasure of surprise may be a low one in the scale; but it is genuine, and not necessarily ignoble. And the same is true of the mere perception of dexterity. To obtain these, on their appropriate occasions, the thousand devices of baroque deceit were invaluable. Humorous or trifling in themselves, they gained an æsthetic interest and dignity because the unity of baroque style allied them to a general scheme.

Besides these ingenuities of the casino, the grotto, and the garden, there were architectural opportunities of a frankly temporary sort. There was the architecture of the *festa*, of the pageant, of the theatre. There was no reason why this should not be serious, supremely imaginative, or curiously beautiful. But it was not required to be, or seem, permanent. There was here no peril of that disappointment, which pretence involves, to the just expectations we form of monumental art. And these occasions, for which the baroque style remains unequalled, were an endless opportunity for architectural experiment. They were the school in which its psychologic skill was trained.

Last, there was monumental architecture. The resources learnt in the theatre must here be subject to restraint. Here we must hold secure our sense of permanence and strength. No falsities, no illusions, can here be tolerated that, when the eye discovers them, will lower our confidence in these qualities. But deceptions which pass unnoticed, and those which have no reference to stability and mass—deceptions of which the psychologic effect is negligible—may even here be admitted. The Parthenon deceives us in a hundred ways, with its curved pediment and stylobate, its inclined and thickened columns. Yet the sense of stability which it gains from these devices survives our discovery of the facts of its construction. The Italian mastery of optics was less subtle than the Greek, but it was put to wider uses. Perhaps the most familiar instance of its employment is in the galleries which connect St. Peter's with the colonnade of Bernini. Here the supposedly parallel lines converge on plan and lengthen the perspective. This, indeed, is by no means a remarkably successful expedient, since what is gained for the eastward perspective is lost in that towards the west. But there is no loss of monumentality. The important point, realised by the architects of this period, is that, even in monumental architecture, the question of 'deceit' is one rather of degree than principle, rather of experiment than law. A design that is in the main substantial, and of which the serious interest is manifest, can 'carry' a certain measure of evident illusion and, needless to say, an indefinite amount of illusion which escapes all detection save that of the plumb-line and measure. An entire façade of false windows may be theatrical. A single such window, especially where its practical necessity is for any reason obvious, lowers in no sense our confidence in the design. Between these extremes the justifiable limits of licence are discoverable only—and were discovered—by experiment.

We have dwelt merely on a few conspicuous examples of the moral judgment in architecture, selecting for defence the worst excesses of the most 'immoral' of the styles. The main principle in all these matters is clear: the æsthetic purpose of the work determines the means to be employed. That purpose might conceivably give a clue to the nature of the artist—to his fundamental tendencies of choice. But we must understand it rightly. The moral judgment, deceived by a false analogy with conduct, tends to intervene before the æsthetic purpose has been impartially discerned. An artist may fail in what he has set before him, his failure may be a moral one, a recognisable negligence, but it is manifested, none the less, in an æsthetic failure, and is only to be discovered for what it is by a knowledge of the æsthetic purpose. It follows that we cannot look to the morality of the artist in his work as a criterion of the æsthetic value of the style.

IV   Thus far it may seem that whenever
the criticism of architecture has taken moral preference as
its conscious principle, it has forthwith led to confusion.
Whether its method has been theological or utilitarian or
intuitive, it has come to the same end: it has raised a prejudice and destroyed a taste without cause, logic, or advantage.

Are we then to say, with the critics on the other side, that
moral issues are utterly different from æsthetic issues, and
expel the moral criticism of architecture, its vocabulary and
its associations, altogether from our thought? For this, we
saw, has been the favourite retort, and this is the method
which those critics who have an exacter sense of architectural technique have tended to adopt.

But among the consequences of the moral criticism of
architecture, not the least disastrous has been its influence
on its opponents.

We have, in fact, at this moment two traditions of criticism. On the one hand there is a tradition in which the
errors examined in this chapter find their soil; a tradition
of criticism constantly unjust, sometimes unctuous, often
ignorant; a tradition, nevertheless, of great literary power.
Into this channel all the currents of the Romantic Fallacy,
all the currents of the Ethical, flow together. It is the Criticism of Sentiment.

On the other hand is a body of criticism sharply opposed
to this. It has two forms: the *'dilettante'*—in the older and
better sense of that word—and the technical: two forms,
different indeed in many respects, but alike in this—that
both are *specialised*, both are learned and exact and in
some sense cynical. They derive their bias and their present character from an obvious cause: a sharp reaction,
namely, against the Criticism of Sentiment. The amateur,
the pedant, the mechanic, have always existed; but, until
the Criticism of Sentiment arose, their exclusiveness was

a matter of temperament and not of creed. On the contrary, the older 'pedants,' with Vitruvius at their head, claimed every kind of moral interest for their art, and were fond of arguing that it involved, and required, a veritable rule of life. But the exacter criticism of our own time, in natural disdain for the false feeling and false conclusions of the opposite school, restricts the scope of architecture to a technical routine, and reduces its criticism to connoisseurship. This, then, is the second tradition: the Criticism of Fact.

The consequences, for the criticism of sentiment, of its lack of exact knowledge and disinterested experience in the art of architecture, have already been set out. But what are the results, for the critics of 'Fact,' of their aversion —historically so justified—to the methods of 'Sentiment'? The results are clear. The appreciation of beauty, cut off from the rest of life, neither illuminates experience, nor draws from experience any profundities of its own. It loses the power to interest others, to influence creation or control taste: it becomes small and desiccated in itself. And another result is equally apparent. Appreciation, thus isolated, discriminates the nice distinctions of *species*, but loses sight of the great distinction of *genus*: the distinction between the profound and the accomplished. An accurate and even interest studies François Boucher with Bellini; an equable curiosity extends itself indifferently to the plans of Bramante and the furniture of Chippendale. For, in the last resort, great art will be distinguished from that which is merely æsthetically clever by a nobility that, in its final analysis, is moral; or, rather, the nobility which in life we call 'moral' is itself æsthetic. But since *it interests us in life as well as in art*, we cannot—or should not—meet it in art without a sense of its imaginative reaches into life. And to separate architecture, the imaginative reach of which has this vital scope—architecture that is profound— from architecture which, though equally accomplished, is nevertheless vitally trivial, is a necessary function even of æsthetic criticism.

There is, in fact, a true, not a false, analogy between ethical and æsthetic values: the correspondence between them may even amount to an identity. The 'dignity' of architecture is the same 'dignity' that we recognise in character. Thus, when once we have discerned it æsthetically in architecture, there may arise in the mind its moral echo. But the echo is dependent on the evoking sound; and the sound in this case is the original voice of architecture, whose language is Mass, Space, Line, and Coherence. These are qualities in architecture which require a gift for their understanding and a trained gift for their understanding aright: qualities in which men were *not* 'intended without excessive difficulty to know good things from bad,' and by no means to be estimated by the self-confident scrutiny of an ethical conscience; qualities, nevertheless, so closely allied to certain values we attach to life, that when once the æsthetic judgment has perceived them rightly, the vital conscience must approve, and by approving can enrich. To refuse this enrichment, or moral echo, of æsthetic values is one fallacy; the fallacy of the critics of Fact. To imagine that because the 'conscience' can enrich those values it has, on that account, the slightest power, with its own eyes, to see them, is the contrary, the Ethical Fallacy of taste.

Morality deepens the content of architectural experience. But architecture in its turn can extend the scope of our morality. This sop, which that Cerberus unchastised shows little disposition to accept, may now be proffered in conclusion.

Values (whether in life or art) are obviously not all compatible at their intensest points. Delicate grace and massive strength, calm and adventure, dignity and humour, can only co-exist by large concessions on both sides. Great architecture, like great character, has been achieved not by a too inclusive grasp at all values, but by a supreme realisation of a few. In art, as in life, the chief problem is a right choice in sacrifices. Civilisation is the organisation of values. In life, and in the arts, civilisation blends a group of compatible values into some kind of sustained and satisfying pattern, for the sake of which it requires great rejections. Civilisation weaves this pattern alike in life and in the arts; but with a difference in the results. The pattern that is realised in conduct is dissipated with each new experiment; the pattern that is realised in art endures.

Our present experiment in democratic ethics may be the best which the facts of life afford: or it may not be the best, and yet be necessary. But, in either case, though morality in action may stand committed to a compromise, the imagination of morality need have no such restrictions. It should have some sense of the values it is forced to subordinate or to reject. Of those values the arts, enduring from the past, retain the impress.

Without the architecture—together with the poetry and other arts—of the Greeks, we should have a poorer conception, even morally, of the possible scope and value of balance and restraint; without the architecture of the eighteenth century, a poorer sense, even morally, of the possible scope and value of coherence—of a fastidious standard consistently imposed; without the architecture of the Renaissance, a far poorer sense of the humanist conviction: the conviction that every value is ideally a good to be utterly explored, and not indolently misprized—the conviction which spurred the Renaissance builders, as it spurred their painters and their thinkers, to attempt, in a sudden and ardent sequence, the extremest poles of opposite design, and in each attempt to discern for a brief instant the supreme and perfect type: a humanist passion which made of architecture the counterpart of all the moods of the spirit, and while, Cortez-like, it laid open the round horizon of possible achievement, never disowned allegiance to a past which it deemed greater than itself.

SIX

The Biological Fallacy

Of all the currents that have lapped the feet of architecture, since architecture fell to its present ruin, the philosophy of evolution must be held to have been the most powerful in its impulse, the most penetrating in its reach. The tide of that philosophy, white with distant promises, is darkened, no less, by the wreckage of nearer things destroyed. Have these waters, then, effaced the characters which, upon the walls of architecture, Romance overlaid with others of its own, Science disfigured, and Ethics sought falsely to restore?

So long as the sequence of Renaissance styles continued unbroken, the standards by which architecture was judged grew and developed with architecture itself. A formative force took possession of critical taste, while it controlled creative power. The large outline of tradition stood fast; but, as within it shape succeeded shape, reason—with due conservative cries and proper protests—yet followed, understood and sanctioned. Style dictated its own criterion; taste accepted it. The past died because the present was alive. Style itself, and not *the succession* of styles, engrossed men's thought. The sequence, *as a sequence*, was not studied. But when, in the nineteenth century, the sequence was cut short and a period of 'revivals' was initiated, the standards of taste were multiplied and confused; past things became contemporary with present. Sequence—the historical relation of style to style—now was studied, when sequence itself had ceased to be. If the different stages of a historical evolution are brought simultaneously to life—if only to the life of chattering spectres—style no longer can affirm its rights unquestioned. Claims that once were owned must then be adjusted, challenged and compared. When architecture, once a clear directing voice, is heard to speak 'with tongues' forgotten and confused, men must hearken for interpretation, and find it, then, in the sound of every passing gust of thought.

Three such sounds in the wind were those we have examined, each of them borne from a source remote from architecture itself. Poetical enthusiasm, the zeal and curiosity of science, the awakened stir of a social conscience, are voices in the criticism of architecture still to be discerned. But the philosophy of evolution—vast in its sweep, universal in its seeming efficacy, and now less an instrument of science than a natural process of the unconscious mind —was a steadier wind more strong than these. What has been its bearing upon the appreciation of Renaissance architecture? Has it assisted us, or not, to see its value as an art and to judge it for that third condition of well-building —its 'delight'? It is the gain and loss which 'evolution' has brought to taste that now must be computed.

In one sense the gain has been obvious. Of the evolutionary influence on criticism the most evident result has been a wide enlargement of our sympathy.

A sharply-defined circle formed the limit of eighteenth-century vision; within it, all was precisely seen, brilliantly illumined; beyond it, outer darkness. That sympathetic traveller, the Président de Brosses, has nothing to say of the paintings of Giotto save that they are 'fort mauvaises'; Goethe, even, at Assisi, does not remark on them at all; nor on the two churches of St. Francis: the vestiges of the classic temple engage all his attention. The architectural histories of the time, after citing a few historic landmarks like the Tower of Babel, hasten on to the business in hand —the 'better manner' of their own day. Step back from 'le grand siècle' and you are in 'le méchant temps.' And when the obligations of devotion compelled these fastidious amateurs to pass an hour beneath a Gothic groin, they took care, at least, that a festive chandelier should hang from it to provide a haven for the outraged eye, and that

richly scrolled and classic woodwork should accommodate
the physical requirements of their piety. Secure in the
merits of 'the better manner' they neither sought, nor were
able, to do justice to the past.

The release from this contracted curiosity was brought
about by two main causes. It was brought about, æsthetically, by the Romantic Movement. It was brought about,
intellectually, by the philosophy of evolution. The Romantic Movement placed a poetic value, for its own sake,
on the remote. The philosophy of evolution, with its impartial interest in all things, placed a scientific emphasis,
for its own sake, upon *sequence*. Both these were enlarge-
ments of our curiosity.

But the Romantic enlargement fails because, although
it finds an æsthetic value in the past, the value it finds is
too capricious and has no objective basis. And the evolutionary enlargement fails because it is not interested in
'value' at all. It does not deny that values exist, but it is of
the essence of its method that it takes no sides—that it
discounts value and disregards it. The intellectual gain is
effectively a loss for art.

The object of 'evolutionary' criticism is, *prima facie*, not
to appreciate but to explain. To account for the facts, not
to estimate them, is its function. And the light which it
brings comes from one great principle: that things are intelligible through a knowledge of their antecedents. *Ex
nihilo nihil fit*; the nature of things is latent in their past.
The myriad forms of architecture fall, by the compulsion
of this principle, into necessary order. The interest of the
study shifts from the terms of the sequence to the sequence
itself. In such a view there is no place for praise or blame.
The most odious characteristics of an art become convenient evidences of heredity and environment, by means of
which every object can be duly set in a grand and luminous
perspective. This tendency of the mind was a needed cor-
rective to the Ethical Criticism; and the clear light of
philosophic calm replaces, in these expositions, the tragic
splendour of denunciatory wraths. Nevertheless, the direc-

tion of the tendency is unmistakable. It is a *levelling* tendency. The less successful moments of the architectural sequence have an equal place with the greatest. More than this, the minor periods, the transitional and tentative phases, acquire, when our interest is centred in the sequence, a *superior* interest to the outstanding landmarks of achieved style. For the intellectual problem is, precisely, to connect these landmarks with one another and with their obscure origins. Hence not in architecture alone, but in many other fields of study—in religion, for instance, and mythology—a sharp prominence is given to what is primitive and submerged, at the expense, inevitably, of the classic points of climax. When there is prominence there is soon prestige. The coldest scrutiny must recognise one value—namely, intellectual *interest*; and interest takes by degrees the place of worth. Thus the ennobled cult becomes for us the bloody sacrifice, civilised usage a savage rite, and the Doric temple justifies its claim on our attention by reminding us that it was once the wooden hut. The question is no longer what a thing ought to be, no longer even what it *is*; but with what it is connected.

But Renaissance architecture is a very unfortunate field for the exercise of this kind of criticism, for the reason, already established, that it was an architecture of taste; an architecture, that is to say, which was not left to develope itself at the blind suasion of an evolutionary law. It cast off its immediate past and, by an act of will, chose—and chose rightly—its own parentage. It scorned heredity; and, if it sometimes reflected its environment, it also did much to create it. It could change its course in mid-career; it was summoned hither and thither at the bidding of individual wills. Brunelleschi, at its birth, searching with Donatello among the ruins of Rome, could undermine tradition. Michael Angelo, independent of the law as Prometheus of Zeus, controlled its progress more surely than did any principle of sequence. And the forces which he set loose, a later will—Palladio's—could stem, and the eighteenth century revoke. Here was no procession of ordered causes, but a pageant of adventures, a fantastic masque of taste.

With what result for criticism? Because Renaissance architecture fits ill into the evolutionary scheme, it is on every side upbraided. Because its will was consciously self-guided, it is called capricious. Because it fails to illustrate the usual lessons of architectural development, it is called unmeaning. Because there is no sequence; because the terms are 'unrelated'—or related not strictly, as in the older styles, by 'evolution'—the terms are *ipso facto* valueless and false. A certain kind of intellectual interest is frustrated: *therefore* æsthetic interest is void. This is the evolutionary fallacy in taste.

At its hands, as at the hands of the Romantic Fallacy, Renaissance architecture suffers by neglect and it suffers by misinterpretation. It suffers by neglect: the historian, committed to his formulas of sequence, is constrained to pass hurriedly by a style which fits them so ill and illustrates them so little. But it suffers also by misinterpretation, for that slight account of the Renaissance style which is vouchsafed is given, as best may be, in the formulas of the rest. It is drilled, with the most falsifying results, into the lowest common terms of an architectural evolution. The prejudice to taste is not merely that facts are studied rather than values; it is not merely that the least worthy facts are studied most, and that the stress falls rather on what is historially illuminating than on what is beautiful. The prejudice is more profound. For evolution was schooled in the study of biology; and historical criticism, when it deals in values at all, tends unconsciously to impose on architecture the values of biology. Renaissance architecture is blamed, in the general, because it is self-guided and 'arbitrary'; yet it is condemned, in the particular, by the unjust dooms of 'necessary' law. Let us take a typical presentation of the style, and see how this occurs.

The architecture of the Renaissance, we are told, and rightly, falls into three fairly distinct periods. There is the period of the Florentine Renaissance—the period of the *quattrocento*—tentative, experimental, hesitating, with a certain naïve quality that makes for charm but hardly for accomplishment: the period of which Brunelleschi is the outstanding figure. Of this manner of building the Pazzi Chapel is the earliest pure example, and the 'Carceri' Church of Giuliano da Sangallo, at Prato, one of the latest. This is the period of immaturity.

The second period is that of Bramante and of Raphael. It is much more sure of itself; its aim is clearly defined and supremely achieved. The tentative Brunelleschian charm has vanished, and a more assured and authoritative manner has taken its place. Here, as at no other time, is struck a complete equipoise between majesty and refinement. The architecture of Bramante and Raphael and Peruzzi is as free from the childish and uncertain prettiness of the work which precedes it as from the 'grossness and carelessness' of that which followed. It shares the faultless ease of the painting of its period. Raphael's ruined villa 'Madama,' Peruzzi's palace of the Massimi, the Farnesina, which these two names dispute, a score of other Roman houses, with that at Florence of the Pandolfini, all have this greatness, this distinction of design. Behind them is discerned the image of the grandest: Bramante's vision of St. Peter's, ill-starred, unrealised.

It is a short period—a single generation well-nigh covers it. But it is the climax of the Renaissance and its prime. It synchronises with the climax of painting and civilisation. It is the architecture of Leo x. and of Leonardo: the architecture of a time that could see its prototype in the assembled genius of the 'School of Athens.' This is the second period of Renaissance architecture: its supreme efflorescence.

And now begins the decline; the perfect equipoise could not be sustained. The inevitable decay sets in. It takes two complementary shapes: exaggeration and vacuity. The noble disposition of architectural forms gives place to restlessness: dignity is puffed into display. The sense of grandeur becomes the greed for size. It is the period of the Baroque: the period of decadence. The problem of style once solved—Bramante's school had solved it—nothing can remain but an abuse of power, and architecture feels the strain of too much liberty. As the architecture of Bramante stood linked to the art of Leonardo, so this of the baroque shares in the general corruption of the time: a time when 'gods without honour, men without humanity, nymphs without innocence, satyrs without rusticity gathered into idiot groups on the polluted canvas and scenic affectations encumbered the streets.' Scenic affectations, broken cornices, triple and quadruple pediments, curved façades, theatrical plans, gesticulating sculpture: everything is irrational, exaggerated, abused. These are the dreams of a collapsing mind; this is the violence of a senile art: a sort of architectural delirium foretelling the approach of death. But senility, if sometimes it is violent, is at other moments apathetic; and the approach of dissolution, if it is heralded by delirium, is foreshadowed also in coma. Thus the third period of the Renaissance is marked sometimes by an opposite mood to its extravagance. The exquisite proportions of Raphael are hardened, in this decline, into academic formulas; architecture, when it is not ostentatious, becomes stiff, rigid, and inert. Simplicity becomes barren, and a restrained taste, vacant. And as the end draws near this vacancy is set in all finality on architecture's features by the Empire style. The Renaissance dies, its thoughts held fixed, by a kind of wandering memory, upon the classic past whence it arose, and which, in its last delusion, it believes itself to have become.

Such is the theme which, in their several manners, our histories repeat. But is it not too good, a little, to be true? Is it not a little like those stories of Herodotus that reveal too plainly the propensity of myth? This perfect image of the life of man—why should we look to find it in the history of architecture? This sequence of three terms—growth, maturity, decay—is the sequence of life as we see it in the organic world, and as we know it in ourselves. To read the events of history and the problems of inanimate fact in the terms of our own life, is a natural habit as old as thought itself. These are obvious metaphors, and literature, which has employed them from the beginning, will not forego their use. It is by words like these that the changes of the world will always be described. But, at least, it might be well to make certain that the description fits the facts. The criticism of architecture, with the solemn terminology of evolution, now too often forces the facts to fit this preconceived description. It is true that of late years a slightly more worthy appreciation of the baroque style—it would be truer to call it a mitigation of abuse than an appreciation—has crept from German into English criticism. But the new, less vivid, colours are still woven on the old pattern. Immaturity, prime, and decay follow one another in predestined sequence. Architecture is still presented to us as an organism with a life of its own, subject to the clockwork of inevitable fate. After Brunelleschi the herald, and Bramante the achiever, must come Bernini and the fall.

Let us retrace the biologic myth. The period of Brunelleschi is tentative and immature—unskilled, but charming. This is true, in a sense, but already it is not exactly true. It asks us to regard Brunelleschi's architecture as a less adept solution of Bramante's problem. It presents him as struggling with imperfect instruments after an ideal which later was fulfilled. We are bound to see his architecture in this light if our thoughts are on the *sequence*. In relation to the sequence, the description may be just. But this precisely was the fallacy of evolution. The values of art do not lie in the sequence but in the individual terms. To Brunelleschi there was no Bramante; his architecture was not Bramante's unachieved, but his own fulfilled. His purpose led to the purpose of Bramante: they were not on that account the same. There is in the architecture of the early Renaissance a typical intention, a desire to please, quite different from Bramante's monumental intention— his desire to ennoble. The immaturity of a child is spent in 'endless imitation' of the maturer world, expressed with unskilled thoughts and undeveloped powers. But the 'immaturity' of the Renaissance was rich with the accumulated skill of the mediæval crafts: it was in some directions—in decorative sculpture, for example—almost too accomplished. And it was not spent in feebly imitating the mature, for the obvious reason that the 'mature' did not yet exist. True, the antique existed; but the Brunelleschian architecture was far from merely imitating the classic architecture of Rome. It had a scale of forms, a canon of proportions and an ideal of decoration that were all its own. The conception of immaturity, therefore, while it is appropriate in one or two respects, is in others misleading; and the parallel is so forced that it were best relinquished.

The first condition of æsthetic understanding is to place ourselves at the point of vision appropriate to the work of art: to judge it in its own terms. But its own terms will probably not be identical with those of the sequence as a whole. If we insist on regarding the sequence, we are forced to compare Brunelleschi with Bramante, and this can only be done in so far as their styles are commensurable—in so far as they have purposes in common. We shall compare them with regard to their command of architectural space and logical coherence, and here, no doubt, Brunelleschi is tentative and immature. But that does not exhaust his individuality: these qualities were not his total aim. The more stress, then, that we lay on the sequence the less justice shall we do to *quattrocento* architecture. The habit of regarding Brunelleschi simply as Bramante's precursor long allowed his genius to remain in shadow. Not so very long ago the assertion of his independent rights, his unrepeated merit, was received as a paradox. He came first in a long sequence, and 'without experience'; how could he, therefore, be supremely great?

The evolutionary criticism which belittled the period of Brunelleschi—and from the same unconscious motive— was something more than just to the period of Bramante: the 'prime and climax' of our architecture's life. Noble as it was in the hands of its finest architects, the central style of the Renaissance had, none the less, its vice. It is too terrified lest it should offend. Bramante, Raphael, Peruzzi,

speak as having authority; but the *style* speaks as the scribes.
A style has the right to be judged at its highest inspiration,
yet, to be fully understood, must be watched at its common task. At moments—but at moments how infrequent!
—this architecture makes concrete, as no other style has
done, the mind's ideal of perfect humanism. But the authentic spirit of Bramante comes to us in how few examples; an element of weakness—an element of philosophy
too rare and too exclusive—withered his inspiration at its
birth. Of all the three stages of the Renaissance sequence,
this central period was the most intensely academic. It
could be as vacant as the Empire style, and as imitative.
The spirit of life which, in spontaneous gaiety, never fails
to play upon the sunny architecture of the *quattrocento*;
the life which in the *seicento* flamed out and gave itself
in prodigal abundance to a thousand ventures; the life
which had been smiling and later laughed aloud, flickers
too often in these intervening years to a dim, elusive spark.
Much that was then built by admired masters—by the
younger Sangallo, for example—would justify the 'evolutionary' strictures, had it been built later. If a servile at-
tendance on the antique is a mark of declining force,
Bramante himself must stand convicted of decadence, for
no imitation is more self-effacing than his domed chapel
of S. Pietro in Montorio. Here is the beauty of an echo:
life, here, is scarcely stirring. The Roman civilisation, in
that favoured moment, was the most brilliant that the Renaissance achieved, the most rounded and complete. But
its architecture, for the most part, had a taint of too much
thought, too incomplete a vigour. We do not seek to argue
it *inferior* to that which followed or preceded: strictly, it is
not comparable with either, and all three have their beauty.
But even if it be preferred above them, the illuminating
fact remains: the weakness that was in it is the weakness
of a 'declining,' a too segregated art; a weakness which, if
it did not thus impertinently intrude into the summer of
the Renaissance, our historians would have signalised as
the chill of its approaching winter.

But, for architecture at least, winter was not approaching—rather, a scorching and resplendent heat. If the evolutionary sequence describes too little accurately the 'climax' and the 'birth,' it is forced to utter travesty for the 'decline.' If decadence means anything at all, it stands for loss of power, loss of self-confidence, loss of grip. It is a failure of the imagination to conceive, of the energy to complete, profound experiments—a wasting away of inherited capital no longer put to interest. The baroque style is the antithesis of all these things. Whatever faults it may have, these are not they. Intellect in architecture has never been more active; the baroque architects rehandled their problem from its base. Where the Brunelleschian architecture and the Bramantesque were static, this was dynamic; where those attempted to distribute perfect balance, this sought for concentrated movement. The expectation of repose, which there had been satisfied at every point, was here deferred, suspended to a climax. Architecture was considered, for the first time, wholly psychologically. So daring a revolution must needs be complex in its issue. The change of principle is so complete, its logic so perfect, that, if we fail to shift the angle of our vision, then virtues which the baroque architects passionately studied, must appear as vices; the very strictness with which they adhered to their æsthetic must seem an obtuse negligence of taste. A dangerous æsthetic, possibly: that is a point which need not here be argued;—but a *decadent* architecture—an architecture that lacked spontaneous force, energy of conception, fertility of invention, or brilliance of achievement—that the baroque style on no fair estimate can be called.

The art of painting—except in so far as it was merely, yet superbly, decorative and in closer subservience to architecture—did, on the contrary, show at this moment a real decline. For the genius of Michael Angelo, which in architecture had merely indicated a line of fruitful advance, had in painting fulfilled, and even passed beyond, the favourable limit. Thus, while the baroque architects were exploring in a veritable fever of invention the possibilities of their inheritance, their contemporaries in painting were marking time, and losing themselves in an empty, facile repetition of past phrases. This is true decadence. So little is it true that the energy of a race rises and falls in ordered sequence that even in artistic activity the most divergent results were simultaneous; and while architecture sprang forward, painting lost its nerve as an individual art, and its sole light was reflected from the conflagrating splendour of baroque architecture.

Even for the Empire style the charge of decadence—though here more plausible—is not convincing. Here, indeed, is displayed a preoccupation with a literary ideal that is never without menace to an art of form. Yet the forms of the style were congruous to a live tradition; they were beautiful; they were consistently applied. The judgment of decadence is here an *ex post facto* judgment. The Empire style did, in fact and as a point of history, mark the dissolution of Renaissance architecture. It had no future; it linked itself to no results. But this might well be accounted for on purely social grounds. A change of patronage in the arts, a profound change in the preoccupation of society, a collapse of old organisations, were necessarily, in France, the sequel of the Revolution and the Napoleonic wars. France, not Italy, was at this moment the holder of the torch of architecture. If the torch fell and was extinguished, we need not argue that it was burnt out.

Decadence is a biological metaphor. Within the field of biology it holds true as a fact, and is subject to law; beyond that field it holds true only by analogy. We can judge an organism by one constant standard—its power to survive: a power that varies in a known progression, a power of supreme importance. But even here—where the sequence of immaturity, prime and decay is a fact governed by predictable law—the power to survive is no test of æsthetic quality: the fragile unfolding of a leaf in spring, its red corruption in autumn, are not less beautiful than its strength in summer. And when we have to deal, not with a true and living organism but with a series of works of art,

the tests of evolution are even more misleading. For here
we ourselves define the unit which we estimate. We have
to be sure that our sequence is really a sequence and not
an accidental group. We have to be sure that there is a
permanent thread of quality by which the sequence may
at every point be judged, and that this quality is at each
point the true centre of the art's intention. The mere
power of an architectural tradition to survive—could we
estimate it—might be a permanent quality but hardly a
relevant one; for the successive moments of an art are self-
justified and self-complete. To estimate one by reference
to another is a dangerous method of criticism. The archaic
stage of an artistic tradition is not mere immaturity of
technique. It implies a peculiar æsthetic aim and conception, and a peculiar relation between the conception and
the technique. In the archaic stage, technique is as a rule
adequate to the conception, and no more: it has no life
of its own; it is no end in itself. And the period of so-called
decadence, so far from showing a decline of technique—
as the organism shows a decline of capacity—is often
marked by a superabundance of technical resources, which
stifle the conception. The atrophy is one of ideas. Our
judgment, then, will have shifted its ground: it will have
estimated one period by its technique, and another by its
conception. And, beyond this, it often falsifies both by re-
lating each of them to the æsthetic purposes of the 'climax' that came between. In recent years it is true the
independent value of archaic art has received a sudden
recognition. To that extent the biological fallacy—at any
rate in painting and sculpture—has been checked. But
then a corresponding injustice is usually done to the later
phases. For the critic's determination to take a comprehensive view, to use inclusive formulas, and to trace an
evolutionary sequence beyond its proper limits, still causes
him to read the whole series of his facts as related to a single
ideal. Such an attitude had compensation when the tradition of architecture was alive, and taste was limited to a
due appreciation of contemporary things; for then appre-

ciation was *so far* perfect, and the past was merely ignored. Taste was specialised at every moment, and developed *pari passu* with creative art. No gift of imaginative flexibility was required. But for a modern criticism, which claims to judge with an impartial eye the whole sequence of architectural history, or even of one single 'style,' that gift, before all others, is demanded. The different æsthetic purposes possible to architecture are not necessarily equally worthy; but before their worth can be estimated it is necessary at least that they should be rightly distinguished and defined. A historical definition of architecture which traces the outward development of form from form will not of itself supply the needed definitions of æsthetic purpose. It will fail to strike the right divisions; it will be too unsubtle, too summary, too continuous. It will be intellectually simple but æsthetically unjust.

Criticism based on historic evolution can no more afford a short cut to the problem of taste than criticism that is based on romantic formulas or on mechanical formulas or on ethical formulas. It is but another case of false simplification: another example of the impatience of the intellect in the presence of a living function that disowns the intellect's authority.

SEVEN

The Academic Tradition

1 'There are in reality,' says architecture's principal historian, 'two styles of Architectural Art—one practised universally before the sixteenth century, and another invented since.' To the former belong 'the true Styles of Architecture,' to the latter 'the Copying or Imitative Styles.' [1]

Renaissance architecture is imitative. It is more imitative than any style of building that preceded it. It went further afield for its models and gave them greater honour. True, it is changeful, various, eager for experiment—this we have already seen: it presses forward. But also, and not less, it glances perpetually back. It has its own problems, but it is concerned, not less, with Greece and Rome. In the Renaissance for the first time the question asked is no longer merely, 'Is this form beautiful or suited?' but, 'Is it *correct?*' For the first time architecture canonised its past.

The outstanding mark of Renaissance architecture is a backward vision, a preoccupation with the antique. So much must be conceded even by those who have studied the variety and realised the vigour which the Renaissance style displays, who see most clearly how inevitable was this imitative impulse and how deep the inventive genius that accompanied it.

But, while this main fact is undeniable, the deductions which criticism has drawn from it are opposite enough. On the one hand it is said, Renaissance architecture, being imitative, has lost touch with life. It is a dead, an artificial, an 'academic' style. It lacks the originality, and it lacks the

[1] Fergusson, *History of Modern Architecture.*

fitness of a style which springs unconsciously to suit a present need, as the mediæval style sprang to suit monastic or
civic institutions, or as the classic styles themselves, fitly
and with originality, suited the ancient state. 'There is not
perhaps a single building of any architectural pretension
erected in Europe since the Reformation . . . which is not
more or less a copy, either in form or detail, from some
building either of a different clime or a different age from
those in which it was erected. There is no building, in fact,
the design of which is not borrowed from some country
or people with whom our only associations are those derived from education alone, wholly irrespective of either
blood or feeling.'[2] That is to say, Renaissance architecture,
like our modern 'revivals,' lacks the merit that belongs to
the natural products of a time and place. *It is too classical.*

On the other hand there is a school of critics who arrive
at a diametrically contrary result. They do not complain
that the Renaissance substitutes the ideal of 'correctness'
for that of fitness and beauty, but that it is *insufficiently*
'correct.' They do not criticise the return to the antique:
they applaud it; but they say that in the early Renaissance
the classic manner was imperfectly mastered, and that in
the later Renaissance it was deliberately misused. They approve Bramante and Palladio and the academic school; but
for the rest—and above all for the baroque—they have one
constant ground of censure: Renaissance architecture per-
verts the forms, and violates the 'rules' of classical design.
It is not classical enough.

Among the prejudices which now affect our vision of
architecture this point of 'imitation' must certainly be
reckoned. Whether for praise or blame, we see, and we
cannot help seeing, the Renaissance style as in some sense
a transcript of classic style. The question is, in what sense?
How are we to view this 'imitation' which for some critics
is too servile, and for others too indifferent?

The answer is not easy, for at first sight the classic in-

[2] Fergusson, *History of Modern Architecture.*

fluence in Renaissance architecture takes wholly different forms. The classicism of Brunelleschi is in spirit a devout obedience to the antique; in result, it produced a style of rare originality. The 'seeker for buried treasure,' as the Romans called him, seeing him day after day bent eagerly among their ruins, returned to Florence to institute an architecture all grace and lightness and charm; slight in the projection of its mouldings, slight in the body of its shafts, and wreathed with slender ornament: a style not rigid or of too strict a rule, seldom massive, and then more after the Etruscan manner than the Roman, and for the most part not massive at all, but lightly pencilled upon space. Yet to adopt the ancient style had been Brunelleschi's purpose, and to have restored it remained his boast. Later, at the height of its self-conscious power, and when, more than at any period, artists of original genius were concentrated in the capital, the Renaissance is satisfied, in architecture, with a merely reproductive effort. The little church of San Pietro in Montorio, already cited—save in a few details, a pagan temple merely—is a work of Bramante at his prime. His project even for St. Peter's is conceived in terms of ancient buildings: it is to raise the Pantheon upon the arches of Constantine's basilica. On the other hand it is in the great reaction when the neo-pagan culture is universally abused, and the academic 'rules' forgotten, that the image of imperial Rome comes, in Christian architecture, most amazingly to a second life. The gates and aqueducts of the emperors, with their proud and classic inscriptions, rise again in the baroque city; the noble planning, the immense vistas, the insolent monuments, the scenic instinct, the grandeur and the scale are all the same. And this architecture, which might have satisfied the dream of Nero, is the work of Sixtus v., the Pope who so hated paganism that he could not look with patience on the sculptures of the Vatican, and in the Belvedere would frown on Venus and Apollo as he passed; who destroyed the ancient ruins which Pius ii. had protected, and valued what he spared only that he might plant upon it the victorious symbol of the cross. And at last, when these extremes of passion and revulsions of style had run their course, and architecture in the eighteenth century had brought classic example and modern needs to a natural consistency, the past once more recalls it to obedience, the Greek style supervenes, and the Renaissance dies after all upon a note of imitative fashion.

Sometimes it is the spirit, sometimes the letter of ancient architecture that the Italian style recalls. Now it indulges its thirst for novelty, and again at intervals does penance in Vitruvian sackcloth. The essence of the classic control is disguised beneath the variety of the forms which manifest it. In what did it consist?

II The return to classic style in building forms part of the general movement of Renaissance Humanism—a phase of culture that touched life at every point and presents everywhere the same strange contradiction, spontaneous in its origin, profound in its consequence, yet in its expression often superficial and pedantic. Pedantry and humanism have in history gone hand in hand; yet humanism in its ideal is pedantry's antithesis.

Humanism is the effort of men to think, to feel, and to act for themselves, and to abide by the logic of results. This attitude of spirit is common to all the varied energies of Renaissance life. Brunelleschi, Macchiavelli, Michael Angelo, Cesare Borgia, Galileo are here essentially at one. In each case a new method is suddenly apprehended, tested, and carried firmly to its conclusion. Authority, habit, orthodoxy are disregarded or defied. The argument is pragmatical, realistic, human. The question, 'Has this new thing a value?' is decided directly by the individual in the court of his experience; and there is no appeal. That is good which is seen to satisfy the human test, and to have brought an enlargement of human power.

Power, in fact—a heightening of the consciousness of power as well as a widening of its scope—was the Renaissance ideal: and Greece and Rome, almost of necessity, became its image and its symbol. The Roman Empire had set the summit of achieved power: the Holy Roman Empire had preserved its memory. The names of Greeks and Romans survived as names of conquest; even Virgil and Ovid were magicians, necromancers, kings. In their words, could the due sorcery be found, power still lay hidden. But most of all, because most visible, the stones which the Romans had built endured into the mediæval world, dwarfing it by their scale and overshadowing it with their dignity. These were tokens of power which all could understand, and their effect upon the awakening mind of the Renaissance may be judged in the sonnets of Du Bellay. Humanism, therefore, inevitably fastened the imagination of architects upon the buildings of Rome.

The Renaissance style, we have already seen, is an architecture of taste, seeking no logic, consistency, or justification beyond that of giving pleasure. In this, clearly, it follows the natural bent of humanism, in its stress on liberty of will. And the baroque manner with its psychological method, its high-handed treatment of mechanical fact and traditional forms, is typically humanistic. But this claim of freedom involved architecture in a dilemma. For every art, and architecture more than any, requires a principle of permanence. It needs a theme to vary, a resisting substance to work upon, a form to alter or preserve, a base upon which, when inspiration flags, it may retire. So long as architectural art was closely linked to utility and to construction, these of themselves provided the permanent element it required. Greek architecture had on the whole observed the logic of the lintel, Gothic the logic of the vault. The restrictions which these constructive principles imposed, the forms which they helped to suggest, were sufficient for design. But when architecture, in the Renaissance, based itself on an experimental science of taste, and refused all extraneous sanctions, it felt for the first time the embarrassment of liberty. Baroque art, as soon as the creative energy deserts it, has nothing to fall back upon. It then becomes (as its failures prove) an unmeaning and aimless force, '*bombinans in vacuo*.'

Architecture, therefore, having denied the absolute authority of use and construction to determine its design, was led to create a new authority in design itself. And since Humanism, with its worship of power, had exalted Rome to an ideal, it was naturally in Roman design that this authority was sought. Roman buildings had to provide not merely an inspiration, but a rule.

Thus the mere æsthetic necessities of the case were sufficient to lead the tentative classicism of Brunelleschi towards the stricter manner of Bramante, and to recall the libertinism of the seventeenth century back to the academic yoke of Palladio.

But other causes, still more powerful, were at work. Three influences, in combination, turned Renaissance architecture to an academic art. They were the revival of scholarship, the invention of printing, the discovery of Vitruvius. Scholarship set up the ideal of an exact and textual subservience to the antique; Vitruvius provided the code: printing disseminated it. It is difficult to do justice to the force which this implied. The effective influence of literature depends on its prestige and its accessibility. The sparse and jealously guarded manuscripts of earlier days gave literature an almost magical prestige, but afforded no accessibility; the cheap diffusion of the printing press has made it accessible, but stripped it of its prestige. The interval between these two periods was literature's unprecedented and unrepeated opportunity. In this interval Vitruvius came to light, and by this opportunity he, more perhaps than any other writer, has been the gainer. His treatise was discovered in the earlier part of the fifteenth century, at St. Gall; the first presses in Italy were established in 1464; and within a few years (the first edition is undated) the text of Vitruvius was printed in Rome. Twelve separate editions of it were published within a century; seven translations into Italian, and others into French and German. Alberti founded his great work upon it, and its influence reached England by 1563 in the brief essay of John Shute. Through the pages of Serlio, Vitruvius subjugated France, till then abandoned to the trifling classicism of François I.; through those of Palladio he became supreme in England. 'Nature, O Emperor,' wrote the Augustan critic, 'has denied me a full stature: my visage is lined with age: sickness has impaired my constitution. . . . Yet, though deprived of these native gifts, I trust to gain some praise through the precepts I shall deliver. I have not sought to heap up wealth through my art. . . . I have acquired but little reputation. Yet I still hope by this work to become known to posterity.' Never was a hope more abundantly fulfilled. Upon this obsequious, short, and unprospering architect the whole glory of antiquity was destined to be concentrated. Europe, for three hundred years, bowed to him as to a god.

The treatise which has so profoundly altered the visible world was indeed exactly designed to fit the temper of the Renaissance. It is less a theory of architecture than an encyclopædia of knowledge, general and particular, in easy combination. 'On the Origin of All Things According to the Philosophers' is the title of one chapter: the next is named 'Of Bricks.' The influence of older Greek treatises is everywhere apparent, particularly in the subtle observations upon optics, and a chapter on acoustics. Æsthetic distinctions are drawn in the manner of the Sophists, and Greek words are constantly employed. On the other hand, the author's first-hand experience is no less obvious, especially in his detailed directions for military architecture. The comprehensive scope of the book answers exactly to the undiscriminating curiosity, at once practical and speculative, by which in the sixteenth and seventeenth century the mind of Europe was devoured. In and out of a vast store of useful, practical advice upon construction and engineering are woven a complacent moral philosophy, some geometry and astronomy, and a good deal of mythical history. We read of the Sun's Course through the

Twelve Signs, and of Ctesiphon's Contrivance for Removing Great Weights. The account of the origin of the Doric Order is quoted by John Shute. It is a simple one: 'And immediately after a wittie man named Dorus (the sonne of Hellen and Optix the Nymphe) invented and made the firste piller drawen to perfection, and called it Dorica.' And the history of the Corinthian Order—a charming fable —satisfied even some of the polished critics of the eighteenth century.[3]

All this was eagerly received, but most eagerly of all were welcomed the famous 'Rules.' 'The capitals must be such that the length and breadth of the abacus are equal to the diameter of the lower part of the column and one eighteenth more; the whole height (including the volute) must be half a diameter. The face of the volutes must recede by one thirty-ninth fraction of the width of the abacus, behind its extreme projection.' And so forth, through all the infinite detail of classic architecture. On those recondite prescriptions the humanist architects fastened; these they quoted, illustrated, venerated, praised; and these they felt themselves at total liberty to disregard.

[3] I quote this story—like the last—in Shute's English: 'After that, in the citie of Corinthe was buried a certaine maiden, after whose burial her nourishe (who lamented much her death) knowing her delightes to have bene in pretye cuppes and suche like conceyts in her life time, with many other proper thinges appertayninge onely to the pleasure of the eye, toke them, and brake them, and put them in a littell preatie baskette, and did sette the basket on her grave, and covered the basket with a square pavinge stone. That done, with weeping tears she sayde, Let pleasure go wyth pleasure; and so the nourishe departed. It chanced that the basket was set upon a certain roote of an herbe called Acanthos, in frenche Branckursine, or bearefote with us. Now in the spring time of the yere, when every roote spreadeth fourth his leaves, in the encreasing they did ronne up by the sides of the basket, until they could ryse no higher for the stone, that covered the basket; and so grew to the fashion that Vitruvius calleth Voluta.' Calimachus of Corinth, passing by, borrowed the idea for the Corinthian Order.

III   For it is too often forgotten by those who assail the influence of Vitruvius, how little in the curiously dual nature of the Renaissance architect the zeal of the scholar was allowed to subjugate the promptings of the artist. True, the zeal of scholarship was there, and it was a new force in architecture; but, fortunately for architecture, the conscience of scholarship was lacking. Pedantry, in that astonishing time, was an ideal; it was an inspiration; it was not a method. Vitruvius helped the architect to master the conventions of an art, of which the possibilities were apprehended but not explored. He wrapt it in the pomp and dignity of learning. But in Italy when he was found at variance with the artist's wishes, his laws were reverently ignored. Even the austere Palladio, when it came to building, permits himself much latitude, and the motive of his written work is far less to propagate the canon of Vitruvius than to make known his own original achievements, which he reckons 'among the noblest and most beautiful buildings erected since the time of the ancients.' Vignola's outlook is no less practical. 'I have used this often, and it is a great success,' he writes against a classic cornice: *riesce molto grata.'* And Serlio, the most ardent Vitruvian of all, admits the charm of novelty.

These were the masters of the academic school. The other camp—the architects of the style which culminated in Borromini—used the classical forms when and how they pleased, as mere raw material for a decorative scheme. They were consumed by a passion for originality that at times became a vice. Whatever their faults—and with the main charges against the baroque we have already dealt—no one could accuse them of imitativeness.

Academic art has its danger. Sometimes it implies a refusal to *rethink* the problem at issue. Sometimes, by a kind of avarice of style, it attempts to make the imagination of the past do service for imagination in the present. But this was not the case in Italy. The difference in the conditions which ancient and modern architecture had to meet, no less than the craving for originality that, after Michael Angelo, became so prominent in the art, were guarantees that the academic formula would not produce sterility. To the energy of Italian architecture, distracted as it was by insistent individualities, made restless with the rapid change of life, split by local traditions and infected always by the disturbing influence of painting, the academic code gave not a barren uniformity but a point of leverage, and a general unity of aim. If some needless pilasters and arid palaces were at times the consequence, the price was not too high to pay.

Outside Italy the value of the academic tradition was different but not less great. Here its function was not to restrain a too impatient and pictorial energy, but to set a standard and convey a method. The Renaissance was an accomplished fact: Europe had turned its back on mediævalism, and looked to Italy for guidance. Italian architecture was the fashion: this was inevitable. But the 'Italian' styles which sprang up in France and England, while they sacrificed the unaffected merits of the old national architecture, were a mere travesty of the foreign. The spirit of fashion, as is commonly the case, seized on the detail and failed to grasp the principle. Ignorant builders, with German pattern books in hand, were little likely to furnish space, proportion and dignity. But capitals and friezes were the authentic mode of Rome. Thus, with an ardent prodigality, little pilasters of all shapes and sizes were lavished, wherever they could find a footing, upon Jacobean mansions and the chateaux of Touraine. But the printed pages of Serlio and Palladio, when they came, were a pledge of orthodoxy. The academic influence rescued the architecture of England and France. It provided a canon of forms by which even the uninspired architect could secure at least a measure of distinction; and genius, where it existed, could be trusted to use this scholastic learning as a means and not an end. Wren, Vanbrugh, and Adam in England,

and the whole eighteenth-century architecture of France, are evidence of the fact.

The value of Vitruvius was relative to a time and place. After three hundred years of exaggerated glory and honest usefulness he became a byword for stupidity. Pope satirised him; archæologists discovered that the Roman buildings corresponded but imperfectly to his laws; the Greek movement dethroned the authority of Rome itself; science turned its back on Greece and Rome together; and Romanticism, with its myth of 'untaught genius,' cast scorn on all codes, rules, and canons whatsoever, and as such.

In this revulsion was born the current prejudice that Renaissance architecture is 'imitative, academic, unalive.' A measure of truth, slight but sufficient to give the prejudice life, underlies the judgment. Fundamentally it is a confusion. An art is academic, in this harmful sense, when its old achievements crush down the energies that press towards the new. But the academic canons of the Renaissance did not represent the past achievements of the Renaissance, but of antiquity. To the Renaissance they were the symbol of an unsatisfied endeavour: the source, consequently, not of inertia, but of perpetual fruitfulness. The pedantry was superficial. Beneath this jargon of the 'Orders'—to us so dead, to them so full of inspiration—the Italian architects were solving a vast and necessary problem. They were leading back European style into the main road of European civilisation—the Roman road which stretched forward and back to the horizon, sometimes overlaid, but not for long to be avoided. They were adapting, enlarging, revivifying the forms of the antique to serve the uses of the modern world. The change was deeply natural. Europe no longer recognised itself in the hopes and habits of its immediate past; it did recognise itself, on the contrary, in that remoter and more civilised society in which it had its origin. The mediæval styles had run their course and outlived their usefulness. To have resisted the logic of events, to have clung to the vestiges of local Gothic— vital and 'rational' as in their time they had been, pic-

turesque and romantic as they are in their survival—this
in truth would have been an artificial act of style. It would
have led, in a few generations, to a state of architecture as
unalive, as falsely academic, as were the shams of archæology three hundred years later.

That Renaissance architecture was built up around an
academic tradition—that it was, in a measure, imitative—
will not, if we understand aright the historical and æsthetic conditions of the case, appear to be a fault. The
academic tradition will, on the contrary, be realised as a
positive force that was natural, necessary, and alive. The
Renaissance architects deviated from the canon whenever
their instinctive taste prompted them to do so; they returned to the canon whenever they felt that their creative
experiment had overreached its profitable bounds. And it
should be realised that a convention of form in architecture has a value *even when it is neglected*. It is present in
the spectator's mind, sharpening his perception of what is
new in the design; it gives relief and accent to the new intention, just as the common form of a poetical metre enables the poet to give full value to his modulations. So, in
Renaissance architecture, a thickening of the diameter of
a column, a sudden increase in the projection of a cornice,
each subtlest change of ratio and proportion, was sure of
its effect. A new æsthetic purpose when it is ready for expression first shows itself and gathers force in a thousand
such deviations, all tending in a sole direction. We may
mark them, for instance, in the early years of the baroque,
and realise how large a factor in their effect lies in the
academic canon which they contradicted.

And if the inherited conventions of architecture assist
the articulation of new style, they serve also to keep keen
the edge of criticism. In Florence the advent of a new
moulding could be the subject of epigrams and sonnets;
the architect who ventured it risked a persecution.[4] The

[4] Cf. the excitement which, according to Milizia, was roused
by Baccio d'Agnolo's treatment of the windows of the Bartolini
Palace. The wrath of the Florentines might, in this case, have

academic tradition ensured that the standard of taste was jealously guarded and critically maintained.

IV   An academic *tradition*, allied, as it was in the Renaissance, to a living sense of art, is fruitful; but the academic *theory* is at all times barren.

The view that, because certain forms were used in the past they must therefore be used without alteration in the future, is clearly inconsistent with any development in architecture. But that idea is, in effect, what the academic theory implies. And our modern cult of 'purity' and 'correctness' in style reposes on the same presumption. 'By a "mistake,"' wrote Serlio, 'I mean to do contrary to the precepts of Vitruvius.' This happens now to sound absurd enough. But it is not more absurd than the taste which insists, in modern building, upon 'pure' Louis XVI. or 'pure' Queen Anne. Certainly every deviation from achieved beauty must justify itself to the eye, and seem the result of deliberate thought, and not of mere ignorance or vain 'originality.' But deviations, sanctioned by thought and satisfying the eye, are the sign of a living art; and the cult of 'correctness' is only to be supported on the assumption that architecture is now, and for ever, a dead contrivance to which our taste and habit must at all costs conform. Consequently, the judgment that Renaissance architecture is 'not classical enough' is as ill-grounded as the judgment that it is 'too classical.'

This meticulous observance of 'pure styles' is a mark of a failing energy in imagination; it is a mark, also, of an inadequacy in thought: of a failure to define the nature of style in general. We cling in architecture to the pedantries of humanism, because we do not grasp the bearing upon architecture of the humanist ideal.

Criticism is in its nature intellectual. It seeks to define

been appeased by a closer acquaintance with the Porta de' Borsari at Verona, where Baccio has a classic precedent.

its subject matter in purely intellectual terms. But taste—the subject matter of criticism—is not purely intellectual. The effort of criticism to 'understand' architecture has done no more than add its own assertions to the confused assertions of mere taste. It has not rendered taste intelligible.

Of this tendency to over-intellectualize architecture we have already traced some typical examples. We have seen architecture reduced to purely mechanical terms, and to purely historical terms; we have seen it associated with poetical ideas, with ideas of conduct and of biology. But, of all forms of criticism, the academic theory which confines architectural beauty to the code of the Five Orders—or to any other code—is the most complete example of this excessive intellectual zeal. It is the most self-conscious attempt that has been made to realise beauty as a form of intellectual order.

Indeed, it is often stated that the beauty of classic architecture resides in Order. And Order, upon analysis, is found to consist in correspondence, iteration, and the presence of fixed ratios between the parts. Ratio, identity, and correspondence form part of the necessary web and fabric of our thought. Reason is compelled to seek them. When it finds them we feel conscious of understanding and control. Order is a desire of the mind; and Order is found in classic architecture. What more natural, then, than to say that architectural beauty—the beauty of classic architecture, at any rate—consists in Order? What higher or more perfect beauty, Plato asked, can exist, than mathematical beauty? And the academic criticism, with its canon of mathematical ratios, enforces the demand.

The intellectual bias of our criticism must be profound which allows this theory to be asserted. For this agreeable fancy—so flattering to the intellect, and so exalted—dissolves at the first brush of experience. It should at once be apparent that Order in design is totally distinct from Beauty. Many of the ugliest patterns and most joyless buildings—buildings from which no being can ever have derived delight—possess Order in a high degree; they exhibit fixed and evident ratios of design. Instances of this among the hideous flats, warehouses and other commercial buildings of our streets require no citation. Here is Order, and no beauty, but, on the contrary, ugliness.

Eighteenth-century critics, perceiving this difficulty, were fond of saying that beauty consisted in 'a judicious mixture of Order and Variety'; and this definition, for want of a better, has been a thousand times repeated. The emendation assists us little, for on the nature of the 'judicious' no light is thrown, save that it lies in a mean between the too much on the one hand, and the too little on the other. And, by a still more fatal oversight, it is not observed that almost every possible gradation of order and variety is found among things admittedly beautiful, and no less among things admittedly ugly. A certain minimum of order is implied in all *design*, good or bad; but, given this, it is clear that what satisfies the eye is not Order, nor a ratio between Order and Variety, but beautiful Order and beautiful Variety, and these in almost *any* combination.

Order, it is allowed, brings intelligibility; it assists our thought. But the act of quickly and clearly perceiving ugliness does not become more pleasant because it is quick, nor the ugliness beautiful because it is evident; and order combined with ugliness serves but to render that ugliness more obvious and to stamp it gloomily upon the mind.

So, too, with proportion. The attempt has constantly been made to discover exact mathematical sequences in beautiful buildings as though their presence were likely either to cause beauty or explain it. The intervals of a vulgar tune are not less mathematical than those of noble music, and the proportions of the human body, which artists like Leonardo (following Vitruvius) sought to describe within a circle and a square, are not most beautiful when they can be exactly related to those figures. It was realised that 'proportion' is a form of beauty: it was realised that 'proportion' is a mode of mathematics. But it was not realised that the word has a different bearing in the two cases.

Criticism is not called upon to invent an æsthetic for disembodied minds, but to explain the preferences which we
(whose minds are not disembodied) do actually possess.
Our æsthetic taste is partly physical; and, while mathematical 'proportion' belongs to the abstract intellect, æsthetic
'proportion' is a preference in bodily sensation. Here, too,
are laws and ratios, but of a different geometry. And there
can be no sure criticism of architecture till we have learnt
the geometry of taste.

Mass, Space, Line, and Coherence constitute, in architecture, the four great provinces of that geometry. When
it has satisfied science with 'firmness,' and common use
with its commodity, architecture, becoming art, achieves,
through these four means, the last 'condition of well-building'—its 'delight.' By the direct agency of Mass and Space,
Line and Coherence upon our physical consciousness, architecture communicates its value as an art. These are the
irreducible elements of its æsthetic method. The problem
of taste is to study the methods of their appeal and the
modes of our response; and to study them with an attention undiverted by the Romantic, Ethical, Mechanical,
Biological or Academic Fallacies of the impatiently con-
cluding mind.

EIGHT

Humanist Values

1 Architecture, simply and immediately perceived, is a combination, revealed through light and shade, of spaces, of masses, and of lines. These few elements make the core of architectural experience: an experience which the literary fancy, the historical imagination, the casuistry of conscience and the calculations of science, cannot constitute or determine, though they may encircle and enrich. How great a chaos must ensue when our judgments of architecture are based upon these secondary and encircling interests the previous chapters have suggested, and the present state of architecture might confirm. It remains to be seen how far these central elements—these spaces, masses and lines—can provide a ground for our criticism that is adequate or secure.

The spaces, masses and lines of architecture, as perceived, are appearances. We may infer from them further facts about a building which are not perceived; facts about construction, facts about history or society. But the art of architecture is concerned with their immediate aspect; it is concerned with them as appearances.

And these appearances are related to human functions. Through these spaces we can conceive ourselves to move; these masses are capable, like ourselves, of pressure and resistance; these lines, should we follow or describe them, might be our path and our gesture.

Conceive for a moment a 'top-heavy' building or an 'ill-proportioned' space. No doubt the degree to which these qualities will be found offensive will vary with the spectator's sensibility to architecture; but sooner or later, if the top-heaviness or the disproportion is sufficiently pronounced, every spectator will judge that the building or the space is ugly, and experience a certain discomfort from their presence. So much will be conceded.

Now what is the cause of this discomfort? It is often suggested that the top-heavy building and the cramped space are ugly because they suggest the idea of instability, the idea of collapse, the idea of restriction, and so forth. But these *ideas* are not in themselves disagreeable. We read the definition of such words in a dictionary with equanimity, yet the definition, if it is a true one, will have conveyed the idea of restriction or collapse. Poetry will convey the ideas with vividness. Yet we experience from it no shadow of discomfort. On the contrary, Hamlet's 'cabined, cribbed, confined' delights us, for the very reason that the idea is vividly conveyed. Nor does Samson painfully trouble *our* peace, when

'Those two massie Pillars
With horrible convulsion to and fro
He tugged, he shook, till down they came and drew
The whole roof after them with burst of thunder
Upon the heads of all who sate beneath.'

Clearly, then, our discomfort in the presence of such architecture cannot spring merely from the idea of restriction or instability.

But neither does it derive from an actual weakness or restriction in our immediate experience. It is disagreeable to have our movements thwarted, to lose strength or to collapse; but a room fifty feet square and seven feet high does not restrict our actual movements, and the sight of a granite building raised (apparently) on a glass shop-front does not cause us to collapse.

There is instability—or the appearance of it; but it is in the building. There is discomfort, but it is in ourselves. What then has occurred? The conclusion seems evident. The concrete spectacle has done what the mere idea could not: it has stirred our physical memory. It has awakened in us, not indeed an actual state of instability or of being overloaded, but that condition of spirit which in the past has belonged to our actual experiences of weakness, of thwarted effort or incipient collapse. We have looked at the building and identified ourselves with its apparent state. *We have transcribed ourselves into terms of architecture.*

But the 'states' in architecture with which we thus identify ourselves need not be actual. The actual pressures of a spire are downward; yet no one speaks of a 'sinking' spire. A spire, when well designed, appears—as common language testifies—to soar. We identify ourselves, not with its actual downward pressure, but its apparent upward impulse. So, too, by the same excellent—because unconscious —testimony of speech, arches 'spring,' vistas 'stretch,' domes 'swell,' Greek temples are 'calm,' and baroque façades 'restless.' The whole of architecture is, in fact, unconsciously invested by us with human movement and human moods. Here, then, is a principle complementary to the one just stated. *We transcribe architecture into terms of ourselves.*

This is the humanism of architecture. The tendency to project the image of our functions into concrete forms is the basis, for architecture, of creative design. The tendency to recognise, in concrete forms, the image of those functions is the true basis, in its turn, of critical appreciation.[1]

[1] The theory of æsthetic here implied, is, needless to say, not new. It was first developed by Lipps twenty years ago, and since then has been constantly discussed and frequently misunderstood.

In what follows I owe a debt to many suggestive points in Mr. Berenson's studies of Italian painting, where this view of æsthetics found its most fruitful concrete application. With this exception the present chapter has been derived wholly from the author's own immediate experience in the study and practice of architecture, and is intended to satisfy rather an architectural than a philosophical curiosity. Time-honoured as Lipps's theory now is, and valid as it appears to me to be, its influence upon purely architectural criticism has been negligible. In English architectural writing it is totally ignored; even Mr. Blomfield, the most philosophical of our critics, gives

    II To this statement several objections may be expected. This 'rising' of towers and 'springing' of arches, it will be said—these different movements which animate architecture—are mere metaphors of speech. No valid inference can be drawn from them. Again, the enjoyment of fine building is a simple and immediate experience, while this dual 'transcription,' by which we interpret the beauty of architecture, is a complicated process. And not only—it will again be objected—is the theory too complicated; it is also too physical. The body, it will be said, plays no part—or a small and infrequent part—in our conscious enjoyment of architecture, which commonly yields us rather an intellectual and spiritual satisfaction than a conscious physical delight. And it will be further said that such a theory is too 'farfetched'; we cannot readily imagine that the great architects of the past were guided by so sophisticated a principle of design. And, if some such process has indeed a place in architecture, it may be doubted finally how far it can account for all the varied pleasures we obtain. It will be convenient to consider these objections at the outset.

The springing of arches, the swelling of domes, and the soaring of spires are 'mere metaphors of speech.' Certainly they are metaphors. But a metaphor, when it is so obvious

it but a frigid welcome. (*The Mistress Art*, p. 118.) Yet its architectural importance, both for theory and practice, is immense; and it is for lack of its recognition that the Fallacies of Criticism still flourish so abundantly. For some theory criticism must have, and in the absence of the true, it makes shift with the palpably false.

I have avoided, as far as clearness seems to permit, all purely psychological discussion. Those interested in this aspect of the matter will find in the recent writings of Vernon Lee the most extensive survey of the question which has appeared in English, together with all necessary references to the foreign literature of the subject.

as to be universally employed and immediately understood, presupposes a true and reliable experience to which it can refer. Such metaphors are wholly different from literary conceits. A merely literary metaphor lays stress on its own ingenuity or felicity. When we read

'Awake, for Morning in the bowl of Night
Has flung the Stone which puts the stars to flight,'

we are first arrested by the obvious disparity between the thing and its description; we then perceive the point of likeness. But when we speak of a tower as 'standing' or 'leaning' or 'rising,' or say of a curve that it is 'cramped' or 'flowing,' the words are the simplest and most direct description we can give of our impression. We do not argue to the point of likeness, but, on the contrary, we are first conscious of the fitness of the phrase and only subsequently perceive the element of metaphor. But art addresses us through immediate impressions rather than through the process of reflection, and this universal metaphor of the body, a language profoundly felt and universally understood, is its largest opportunity. A metaphor is, by definition, the transcription of one thing into terms of another, and this in fact is what the theory under discussion claims. It claims that architectural art is the transcription of the body's states into forms of building.

The next point is more likely to cause difficulty. The process of our theory is complex; the process of our felt enjoyment is the simplest thing we know. Yet here, too, it should be obvious that a process simple in consciousness need not be simple in analysis. It is not suggested that we *think* of ourselves as columns, or of columns as ourselves. No doubt when keen æsthetic sensibility is combined with introspective habit, the processes of transcription will tend to enter the field of consciousness. But there is no reason why even the acutest sensibility to a resultant pleasure should be conscious of the processes that go to make it. Yet some cause and some process there must be. The processes of which we are least conscious are precisely the most deep-seated and universal and continuous, as, for example, the process of breathing. And this habit of projecting the image of our own functions upon the outside world, of reading the outside world in our own terms, is certainly ancient, common, and profound. It is, in fact, the *natural* way of perceiving and interpreting what we see. It is the way of the child in whom perpetual pretence and 'endless imitation' are a spontaneous method of envisaging the world. It is the way of the savage, who believes in 'animism,' and conceives every object to be invested with powers like his own.[2] It is the way of the primitive peoples, who in the elaborate business of the dance give a bodily rendering to their beliefs and desires long before thought has accurately expressed them. It is the way of a superbly gifted race like the Greeks, whose mythology is one vast monument to just this instinct. It is the way of the poetic mind at all times and places, which humanises the external world, not in a series of artificial conceits, but simply so perceiving it. To perceive and interpret the world scientifically, as it actually is, is a later, a less 'natural,' a more sophisticated process, and one from which we still relapse even when we say the sun is rising. The scientific perception of the world is forced upon us; the humanist perception of it is ours by right. The scientific method is intellectually and practically useful, but the naïve, the anthropomorphic way which humanises the world and interprets it by analogy with our

[2] Thus it has of late been more fully realised that children and primitive races are often capable of very remarkable achievement in expressive art, while the scientific perception of the world for the most part undermines the gift. If the child or the savage is incapable of appreciating great architecture, it is not because they lack the æsthetic sense (for a child the general forms, for instance, of a piece of furniture are often charged with significance and impressiveness), but because the scope and continuity of their attention is too limited to organise these perceptions into any æsthetic whole, still more to give them concrete realisation. None the less, it is on this half-conscious or subconscious, yet not quite undiscoverable world in which, more than ourselves, they live, that architecture, like all the arts, depends for its effect.

own bodies and our own wills, is still the æsthetic way; it
is the basis of poetry, and it is the foundation of architecture.

A similar confusion between what is conscious in architectural pleasure, and what is merely implied, seems to un-
derlie the objection that our theory lays too great a stress
on physical states. Our pleasure in architecture, it is true,
is primarily one of the mind and the spirit. Yet the link
between physical states and states of the mind and the
emotions needs no emphasis. Our theory does not say that
physical states enter largely into the spectator's consciousness; it says that they, or the suggestion of them, are a
necessary precondition of his pleasure. Their absence from
consciousness is indeed a point of real importance. Large
modifications in our physical condition, when they occur,
alter our mental and emotional tone; but, also, they absorb
our consciousness. A person, for example, who is taking
part in an exciting game, will feel exhilaration and may
enjoy it; but the overtones of gaiety, the full intellectual
and emotional interest of the state, are drowned in the
physical experience. The mind is not free to attend to them.
It is precisely because the *conscious* physical element in
architectural pleasure is so slight, our imitative self-adjust-
ment to architectural form so subtle, that we are enabled
to attend wholly to the intellectual and emotional value
which belongs to the physical state. If we look at some
spirited eighteenth-century design, all life and flicker and
full of vigorous and dancing curves, the physical echo of
movement which they awaken is enough to recall the appropriate mental and emotional penumbra; it is not sufficient to overwhelm it. No one has suggested that the experiences of art are as violent or exciting as the experiences
of physical activity; but it is claimed for them that they are
subtler, more profound, more lasting, and, as it were, possessed of greater resonance. And this difference the theory
we are considering assists us to understand.

Any explanation of the workings of the æsthetic instinct, however accurate, must inevitably have a modern

ring. It must seem incongruous when applied to the artists of the past, for the need and the language of such explanations are essentially of our own day. It would not therefore—to pass to the next objection—be a serious obstacle to our theory if the conception of architecture, as an art of design based on the human body and its states, had been wholly alien to the architects of the past. But this is not altogether the case. The Renaissance architects were, in fact, frequently curious to found their design upon the human body, or, rather, to understand how the human body entered into the current traditions of design. Among their sketches may be found some where the proportions of the male form are woven into those of an architectural drawing and made to correspond with its divisions. An elaborate, though uninspired, rendering of the Tuscan, Ionic, and Corinthian Orders into human forms was published by John Shute in the earliest printed work on architecture in England. And in this connection the ancient, though seldom felicitous, habit of actually substituting caryatides and giants for the column itself is not without significance. It was realised that the human body in some way entered into the question of design. But habits of thought were at that time too objective to allow men any clear understanding of a question which is, after all, one of pure psychology. What they instinctively apprehended they had no means intellectually to state; and that correspondence of architecture to the body, which was true in abstract principle, they sometimes vainly sought to prove in concrete detail. Thus they looked in architecture for an actual reproduction of the proportion and symmetries of the body, with results that were necessarily sometimes trivial and childish. Vasari was nearer the truth when he said in praise of a building that it seemed 'not built, but born'— *non murato ma veramente nato*. Architecture, to communicate the vital values of the spirit, must appear organic like the body. And a greater critic than Vasari, Michael Angelo himself, touched on a truth more profound, it may be, than he realised, when he wrote of architecture: 'He that hath not mastered, or doth not master the human figure, and in especial its anatomy, may never comprehend it.'

    III But, how far, it is natural to ask, can such an explanation be carried? Granting its truth, can we establish its sufficiency? Our pleasure in architectural form seems manifold. Can one such principle explain it? A full answer to this question is perhaps only to be earned in the long process of experiment and verification which the actual practice of architecture entails. How minutely Humanism can enter into the detail of architecture, how singularly it may govern its main design, could not, in any case, be demonstrated without a mass of instances and a free use of illustration. A study of these, drawn from Renaissance architecture, could form the matter of another volume. But the main divisions of the subject—space, mass, line and coherence, with their more obvious applications—may here be singled out.

  The principle is perhaps most clearly to be recognised in *line*. Lines of one sort or another always form a large part of what is visually presented to us in architecture. Now in most cases, when we bring our attention to bear on one of these lines, its whole extent is not seen with absolute simultaneity; we 'follow' it with our eye. The mind passes successively over points in space, and that gives us movement. But when we have got movement we have got expression. For our own movements are the simplest, the most instinctive, and the most universal forms of expression that we know. Identified with ourselves, movement has meaning; and line, through movement, becomes a gesture, an expressive act. Thus, for example, the curves of a volute are recognised as bold or weak, tense or lax, powerful, flowing, and so forth. It is by such terms as these, in fact, that we praise or condemn them. But we must recognise them as having these qualities by unconscious analogy with our own movements, since it is only in our own bodies that we know the relation of the line—or movement—to the feeling it denotes.

Movement is most obviously communicated by curved lines; but it is conveyed also by lines which are straight. No doubt the straight lines which bound the rectangular forms of architecture, its doors and its windows, are chiefly realised, not as sensations in themselves, but as definitions of the shapes they enclose. Their chief use is to determine the position of a patch upon a given surface; and the æsthetic value of this will be considered in a moment. But any emphasis upon vertical lines immediately awakens in us a sense of upward direction, and lines which are spread— horizontal lines—convey suggestions of rest. Thus the architect has already, in the lines of a design, a considerable opportunity. He controls the path of the eye; the path we follow is our movement; movement determines our mood.

But line is not the sole means of affecting our sense of movement. Space, also, controls it. Spaces may be in two dimensions or in three. We may consider the simpler case first. A large part of architectural design consists in the arrangement of forms upon surfaces, that is to say, within spaces. The part which movement here plays will be clear from a common instance. A man who is arranging pictures on a wall will say that one is 'crowded' or 'lost' in the space it occupies, that it 'wants to come' up or down. That is to say, the position of forms upon a surface is realised in terms of our physical consciousness. If a certain patch 'wants to come' down, we ourselves, by our unconscious imitation of it, have the sense of a perpetually thwarted instinct of movement. The arrangement of the scheme is imperfectly *humanised*. It may be picturesque, it may be useful, it may be mechanically superior; but it is at variance with our ideal movement. And beauty of disposition in architecture, like beauty of line, arises from our own physical experience of easy movement in space.

But not all movements are pleasant or unpleasant in themselves; the majority of them are indifferent. Nevertheless, a *series* of suggested movements, in themselves indifferent, may awaken in us an expectancy and consequent desire of some further movement; and if the spaces of architecture are so arranged as first to awaken and then falsify this expectation, we have ugliness. For example, if a design be obviously based on symmetry and accustoms us to a rhythm of equal movements—as in the case of a typical eighteenth-century house—and one of the windows were placed out of line and lower than the rest, we should feel discomfort. The offence would lie against our sense of a movement, which, when it reaches that point of a design, is compelled to drop out of step and to dip against its will. Yet the relation of the window to its immediately surrounding forms might not in itself be necessarily ugly.

A converse instance may here be given. Classic design —the style which in Italy culminated in Bramante—aims at authority, dignity, and peace. It does this by conveying at every point a sense of equipoise. The forms are so adjusted amid the surrounding contours as to *cancel all suggested movement*: they are placed, as it were, each at the centre of gravity within the space, and our consciousness is thus sustained at a point of rest. But the baroque architects rejected this arrangement. They employed space adjustments which, *taken in isolation,* would be inharmonious. In their church façades, as Wölfflin has pointed out, they quite deliberately congested their forms. The lower windows are jammed between the pilasters on either side; they are placed above the centre of gravity; they give the sense of lateral pressure and upward movement. This, taken alone, would leave us perpetually in suspense. But in the upper part of the design our expectancy is satisfied; the upward movement is allowed to disperse itself in greater areas of lateral space, and makes its escape in a final flourish of decorative sculpture; or it is laid to rest by an exaggerated emphasis upon the downward movement of the crowning pediment and on the horizontals of the cornice. Here, therefore, a movement, which in the midst of a Bramantesque design would be destructive and repugnant, is turned to account and made the basis of a more dramatic, but not less satisfying treatment, the motive of which is not peace, but energy.

IV But besides spaces which have merely length and breadth—surfaces, that is to say, at which we look—architecture gives us spaces of three dimensions in which we stand. And here is the very centre of architectural art. The functions of the arts, at many points, overlap; architecture has much that it holds in common with sculpture, and more that it shares with music. But it has also its peculiar province and a pleasure which is typically its own. It has the monopoly of space. Architecture alone of the Arts can give space its full value. It can surround us with a void of three dimensions; and whatever delight may be derived from that is the gift of architecture alone. Painting can depict space; poetry, like Shelley's, can recall its image; music can give us its analogy; but architecture deals with space directly; it uses space as a material and sets us in the midst.

Criticism has singularly failed to recognise this supremacy in architecture of spatial values. The tradition of criticism is practical. The habits of our mind are fixed on matter. We talk of what occupies our tools and arrests our eyes. Matter is fashioned; space comes. Space is 'nothing'—a mere negation of the solid. And thus we come to overlook it.

But though we may overlook it, space affects us and can control our spirit; and a large part of the pleasure we obtain from architecture—pleasure which seems unaccountable, or for which we do not trouble to account—springs in reality from space. Even from a utilitarian point of view, space is logically our end. To enclose a space is the object of building; when we build we do but detach a convenient quantity of space, seclude it and protect it, and all architecture springs from that necessity. But æsthetically space is even more supreme. The architect models in space as a sculptor in clay. He designs his space as a work of art; that is, he attempts through its means to excite a certain mood in those who enter it.

What is his method? Once again his appeal is to Movement. Space, in fact, is liberty of movement. That is its value to us, and as such it enters our physical consciousness. We adapt ourselves instinctively to the spaces in which we stand, project ourselves into them, fill them ideally with our movements. Let us take the simplest of instances. When we enter the end of a nave and find ourselves in a long vista of columns, we begin, almost under compulsion, to walk forward: the character of the space demands it. Even if we stand still, the eye is drawn down the perspective, and we, in imagination, follow it. The space has suggested a movement. Once this suggestion has been set up, everything which accords with it will seem to assist us; everything which thwarts it will appear impertinent and ugly. We shall, moreover, require something to close and satisfy the movement—a window, for example, or an altar; and a blank wall, which would be inoffensive as the termination of a symmetrical space, becomes ugly at the end of an emphasised axis, simply because movement without motive and without climax contradicts our physical instincts: it is not humanised.

A symmetrical space, on the other hand, duly proportioned to the body—(for not *all* symmetrical spaces will be beautiful)—invites no movement in any one direction more than another. This gives us equipoise and control; our consciousness returns constantly to the centre, and again is drawn from the centre equally in all directions. But we possess in ourselves a physical memory of just the movement. For we make it every time we draw breath. Spaces of such a character, therefore, obtain an additional entry to our sense of beauty through this elementary sensation of expansion. Unconscious though the process of breathing habitually is, its vital value is so emphatic that any restriction of the normal function is accompanied by pain, and—beyond a certain point—by a peculiar horror; and the slightest assistance to it—as, for example, is noticed in high air—by delight. The need to expand, felt in all our bodily movements, and most crucially in breathing, is not only profound in every individual, but obviously of infinite antiquity in the race. It is not surprising, then, that it should have become the body's veritable symbol of well-being, and that spaces which satisfy it should appear beautiful, those which offend it ugly.

We cannot, however, lay down fixed proportions of space as architecturally right. Space value in architecture is affected first and foremost, no doubt, by actual dimensions; but it is affected by a hundred considerations besides. It is affected by lighting and the position of shadows: the source of light attracts the eye and sets up an independent suggested movement of its own. It is affected by colour: a dark floor and a light roof give a totally different space sensation to that created by a dark roof and a light floor. It is affected by our own expectancy: by the space we have immediately left. It is affected by the character of the predominating lines: an emphasis on verticals, as is well known, gives an illusion of greater height; an emphasis on horizontals gives a sense of greater breadth. It is affected by projections—both in elevation and in plan—which may cut the space and cause us to feel it, not as one, but several. Thus, in a symmetrical domed church it will depend on the relation of the depth of the transepts to their own width, and to that of the span of the dome, whether we experience it as one space or as five; and a boldly projecting cornice may set the upward limit of space-sensation instead of the actually enclosing roof.

Nothing, therefore, will serve the architect but the fullest power to *imagine* the space-value resulting from the complex conditions of each particular case; there are no liberties which he may not sometimes take, and no 'fixed ratios' which may not fail him. Architecture is not a machinery but an art; and those theories of architecture which provide ready-made tests for the creation or criticism of design are self-condemned. None the less, in the beauty of every building, space-value, addressing itself to our sense of movement, will play a principal part.

v If voids are the necessary medium of movement, solids are the essential instrument of support; and a dependence upon physical firmness and security is not less fundamental to our nature than that instinctive need for expansion which gives value to architectural space. Any unlooked-for failure of *resistance* in tangible objects defeats the vital confidence of the body; and if this were not already obvious, the pervasive physical disquiet which the mildest tremor of earthquake is sufficient to excite, might show how deeply organised in our nature is our reliance upon the elementary stability of mass. Weight, pressure and resistance are part of our habitual body experience, and our unconscious mimetic instinct impels us to identify ourselves with apparent weight, pressure, and resistance exhibited in the forms we see. Every object, by the disposition of the bulk within its contours, carries with it suggestions of weight easily or awkwardly distributed, of pressures within itself and upon the ground, which have found—or failed to find—secure and powerful adjustment. This is true of any block of matter, and the art of sculpture is built upon this fact. But when such blocks are structurally combined, complex suggestions of physical function are involved—greater in number, larger and more obvious in scale. Architecture selects for emphasis those suggestions of pressure and resistance which most clearly answer to, and can most vividly awaken, our own remembrance of physical security and strength. In the unhumanised world of natural forms, this standard of our body is on all hands contradicted. Not only are we surrounded by objects often weak and uncompacted, but also by objects which, being strong, are yet not strong in our own way, and thus incapable of raising in ourselves an echo of their strength. Nature, like the science of the engineer, requires from objects such security and power as shall in fact be necessary to each; but art requires from them a security and power which shall resemble and confirm our own. Architecture, by the value of mass, gives to solid forms this human adequacy, and satisfies a vital instinct in ourselves. It exacts this adequacy in the detail of its decoration, in the separate elements that go to make its structure, in the structure itself, and in the total composition. The Salute at Venice—to take a single instance—possesses the value of mass in all these particulars. The sweeping movement suggested by the continuous horizontal curve of the Grand Canal is brought to rest by the static mass of the church that stands like its gate upon the sea. The lines of the dome create a sense of massive bulk at rest; of weight that loads, yet does not seem to crush, the church beneath; as the lantern, in its turn, loads yet does not crush the dome. The impression of mass immovably at rest is strengthened by the treatment of the sixteen great volutes. These, by disguising the abrupt division between the dome and church, give to the whole that unity of bulk which mass requires. Their ingenious pairing makes a perfect transition from the circular plan to the octagonal. Their heaped and rolling form is like that of a heavy substance that has slidden to its final and true adjustment. The great statues and pedestals which they support appear to arrest the outward movement of the volutes, and to pin them down upon the church. In silhouette the statues serve (like the obelisks of the lantern) to give a pyramidal contour to the composition, a line which more than any other gives mass its unity and strength. Save for a few faults of design in the lower bays, there is hardly an element in the church which does not proclaim the beauty of mass, and the power of mass to give essential simplicity and dignity even to the richest and most fantastic dreams of the baroque.

In architecture, then, the principal conditions of mass are these. In the first place the effect of the whole must predominate over that of the parts; the parts must en-

force the general character of the whole and help us
to realise its bulk; they must not detach themselves from
the mass in such a way as to detract from its apparent unity.
This, for example, is the ground of the Renaissance insistence upon crowning cornices and other devices for tying
the elements of a building, and forcing it as a single impression on the eye.

Secondly, the disposition of the whole must conform to
our sense of powerfully adjusted weight. Hence the careful
study which the baroque architects gave to the effect of
receding planes, and the influence of upward perspective
upon mass. Hence also, obviously, the use of rusticated
bases, battered plinths, pyramidal composition and the
subordination of the Doric to the lighter Ionic and Corinthian Orders.

Finally, it is necessary that the several parts of a building
should be kept in proper 'scale.' Scale, in any design, is
that relation of ornament (or minor features) to the larger
elements, which controls our impression of its size. In any
building three things may be distinguished: the bigness
which it actually has, the bigness which it appears to have,
and the feeling of bigness which it gives. The two last have
often been confused, but it is the feeling of bigness which
alone has æsthetic value. It is no demerit in a building
that it should fail (as St. Peter's is said to fail) to 'look its
size.' For big things are not, as such, more beautiful than
small, and the smallest object—a mere gem for example—
if it satisfies the three conditions just stated, may convey a
feeling of dignity, mass, and largeness. On the other hand,
a building which looks big may fail to convey a *feeling* of
bigness. No one, for instance, looking at the new Museum
at South Kensington, could fail to realise that its dimensions are vast; it looks its size. But the whole does not
predominate over the parts, the parts are many and the
scale is small. Hence, while we perceive this building to be
large, it conveys a feeling not of largeness, but of smallness
multiplied.

Small scale, no less than large, may be employed to

emphasise effects of mass, as, for example, when fine mouldings are used in combination with large, unbroken surfaces. In transcribing ourselves into such a building we instinctively take its detail as our unit of measurement, and this gives us an increased sense of the grandeur and simplicity of the unbroken mass. Broadly speaking the *quattrocento* architects employed this method, while the baroque architects sought to emphasise mass by the magnitude of the parts themselves. But in both cases the conditions of success were the same: the whole must predominate over the parts, the weight seem powerfully adjusted, the scale be consistently maintained.

VI The humanist instinct looks in the world for physical conditions that are related to our own, for movements which are like those we enjoy, for resistances that resemble those that can support us, for a setting where we should be neither lost nor thwarted. It looks, therefore, for certain masses, lines, and spaces, tends to create them and recognise their fitness when created. And, by our instinctive imitation of what we see, their seeming fitness becomes our real delight.

But besides these favourable physical states, our instinct craves for order, since order is the pattern of the human mind. And the pattern of the mind, no less than the body's humour, may be reflected in the concrete world. Order in architecture means the presence of fixed relations in the position, the character and the magnitude of its parts. It enables us to interpret what we see with greater readiness; it renders form intelligible by making it coherent; it satisfies the desire of the mind; it humanises architecture.

Nevertheless order, or coherence, in architecture stands on a different plane to the values of mass, space, and line; for these, of themselves, give beauty, while order (as was shown in the last chapter) is compatible with ugliness. Yet it is clear that in all the architecture which descends from

Greece and Rome, order plays a principal part. What then is its place and function?

Order—a presence of fixed ratios—will not give beauty, nor will a mixture of order and variety, but so much order, merely, and of such a kind, as is necessary for the effects which humanised mass and space and line are at any point intended to convey. Thus, in making the masses, spaces, and lines of architecture respond to our ideal movement and ideal stability, a measure of symmetry and balance are constantly entailed. Not perfect symmetry, necessarily. We in our bodies have a sense of right and left, and instinctively require that architecture should conform to this duality. Without it we could not so smoothly read or interpret architecture in our own terms. Dissymmetry in an object involves an emphasis or inclination to one side or the other in the movement it suggests, and this sometimes may be appropriate to the mood of the design. But, whenever architecture seeks to communicate the pleasure of equipoise and calm, or to impart a sense of forward, unimpeded movement, symmetrical composition and axial planning must result. Symmetry and Balance are forms of Order; but they are beautiful, not because they are orderly, but because they carry with them a movement and stability which are our natural delight. Then, since architecture is a monumental art, surrounding us with an influence never relaxed and not to be escaped, calm and unthwarted movement will here most often be desired. Thus Order, though it cannot ensure beauty, may follow in its wake.

Yet Coherence in architecture, distinct though it is from beauty, has a function of its own. Humanised mass, space, and line are the basis of beauty, but coherence is the basis of style. Mass, space, and line afford the material of individual æsthetic pleasures, of beauty isolated and detached. But architecture aims at more than isolated pleasures. It is above all else an art of synthesis. It controls and disciplines the beauty of painting, sculpture, and the minor arts; it austerely orders even the beauty which is its own. It seeks, through style, to give it clarity and scope, and that coherence which the beauty of Nature lacks. Nature, it is true, is for science an intelligible system. But the *groups* which the eye, at any one glance, discovers in Nature are not intelligible. They are understood only by successive acts of attention and elimination; and, even then, we have to supplement what our vision gives us by the memory or imagination of things not actually seen. Thus, Order in Nature bears no relation to *our* act of vision. It is not humanised. It exists, but it continually eludes us. This Order, which in Nature is hidden and implicit, architecture makes patent to the eye. It supplies the perfect correspondence between the act of vision and the act of comprehension. Hence results the law of coherence in architecture; what is simultaneously seen must be simultaneously understood. The eye and the mind must travel together; thought and vision move at one pace and in step. Any breach in continuity, whether of mood or scale, breaks in upon this easy unison and throws us back from the humanised world to the chaotic. The values of mass, space, and line are as infinite as the moods of the spirit, but they are not to be simultaneously achieved, for they are mutually conflicting. Style, through coherence, subordinates beauty to the pattern of the mind, and so selects what it presents that all, at one sole act of thought, is found intelligible, and every part re-echoes, explains, and reinforces the beauty of the whole.

Of all the styles of building that yet have been created, the forms of Greece and Rome, with those of the Renaissance after them, were in this point the most exact and strict. They are by consequence the fittest instruments for giving clarity to sharp ideas, however varied, of function and of scale. Other instruments, doubtless, there will be in the future. For if the scope of classical design could be perpetually enlarged until the eighteenth century, it is not probable that its history is closed. But first we must discard a century of misplaced logic. Architecture must be perceived sensitively but simply; the 'theories' of the art have blunted sensitive perception without achieving intellectual force. Architecture that is spacious, massive and coherent, and whose rhythm corresponds to our delight, has flourished most, and most appropriately, at two periods, antiquity and the period of which antiquity became the base—two periods when thought itself was humanistic. The centre of that architecture was the human body; its method, to transcribe in stone the body's favourable states; and the moods of the spirit took visible shape along its borders, power and laughter, strength and terror and calm. To have chosen these nobly, and defined them clearly, are the two marks of classic style. Ancient architecture excels in perfect definition; Renaissance architecture in the width and courage of its choice.

NINE

Conclusion

Such are the four great elements of build-
ing from whose laws the finest masters of the Renaissance,
however various their impulse and achievement, did not
deviate. Theirs is an architecture which by Mass, Space and
Line responds to human physical delight, and by Coherence answers to our thought. These means sufficed them.
Given these, they could dispense at will with sculpture and
with colour, with academic precedents and poetic fancies,
with the strict logic of construction or of use. All those,
also, they could employ: but by none of them were they
bound. Architecture, based on Humanism, became an independent art.

Architecture a humanised pattern of the world, a scheme
of forms on which our life reflects its clarified image: this
is its true æsthetic, and here should be sought the laws—
tentative, at first, but still appropriate—of that third 'condition of well-building,' its 'delight.' To combine these
'laws of delight' with the demands of 'firmness' and 'commodity' is a further problem: in fact the practical problem
of the architect. To trace how this union has been achieved,
and by what concessions, is the task of the historian. But
these three studies are distinct. And the crucial, the central,
function of architectural criticism is the first.

This principle of humanism explains our pleasure in
Renaissance building. It gives us, also, some final links that
we require. It forms the common tie between the different
phases—at first sight so contradictory—of Renaissance style.
It accounts for its strange attitude, at once obsequious and
unruly, to the architecture of antiquity. It explains how

Renaissance architecture is allied to the whole tendency of thought with which it was contemporary—the humanist attitude to literature and life.

Man, as the savage first conceived him, man, as the mind of science still affirms, is not the centre of the world he lives in, but merely one of her myriad products, more conscious than the rest and more perplexed. A stranger on the indifferent earth, he adapts himself slowly and painfully to inhuman nature, and at moments, not without peril, compels inhuman nature to his need. A spectacle surrounds him—sometimes splendid, often morose, uncouth and formidable. He may cower before it like the savage, study it impartially for what it is, like the man of science; it remains, in the end, as in the beginning, something alien and inhuman, often destructive of his hopes. But a third way is open. He may construct, within the world as it is, a pattern of the world as he would have it. This is the way of humanism, in philosophy, in life, and in the arts.

The architecture of humanism rose in Greece; and of the Greeks it has been said that they first made man 'at home in the world.' Their thought was anthropocentric: so also was their architecture. Protagoras, who first made humanity the centre of a metaphysic, and 'the measure of all things'; the poets who, in the labours of Heracles and Theseus and the strife of the gods with centaurs, celebrated the conquest by human reason of a corner in the darkened world; Socrates, who drew down speculation from the flattery of the stars to the service of the conscience; the dramatists, who found tragedy a savage rite and left it a mirror of life, not as it is but as our mind demands: these were the first humanists. Among these men, and to satisfy this same proclivity, was created an architecture whose several elements were drawn indeed from primitive necessities, but so ordered and so chosen that its constructive need and coarse utility were made to match the delight of the body and mock the image of the mind. Matter—the very antithesis of spirit—matter with its mere weight and mass and balance; space, the mere void we recognise as nothing, became, for them, the spirit's language. Within the world of concrete forms indifferent to man, they constructed a world as man desires it, responsive to his instinct and his stature.

But humanism has its practical aspect as well as its ideal; and the values which the Greek defined and founded, the Roman fixed impregnably upon the earth. Roman architecture, less fastidious than the Greek, and less restricted, preserved the principles of mass, space, line and coherence for rougher uses, wider and more general. It ensured their survival, their independence of the time and place whence they had sprung. In architecture as in thought it is to Rome, not Greece, that humanism owes its deep and racial hold upon the West.

The architecture which thus rose with humanism was with humanism eclipsed and with humanism restored. To pass from Roman architecture or that of the Renaissance to the fantastic and bewildered energy of Gothic, is to leave humanism for magic, the study of the congruous for the cult of the strange. It is to find that the logic of an inhuman science has displaced the logic of the human form. It is to discover resplendent beauty of detail in glass and bronze and ivory and gold; it is to lose architecture in sculpture. Here is structure, certainly—daring, intricate, ingenious; but seldom humanised structure. Here is poetry, curious craftsmanship, exquisite invention. But the supreme, the distinctive quality of architecture—that pure identity between the inner and the outer world—is unattempted. The lines of this amazed construction are at one moment congruous with our movement, at the next they contradict it with a cramped and angular confusion. Mass is too often lost in multiplicity. Space and coherence come, if at all, unsought and unregarded; and when they come it is most often because the ritual of the Church, preserving something of the pagan order it inherits, imposed a harmony upon the plan. Divorced from this ritual, Gothic, as its domestic building and its streets suffice to prove, admits its deep indifference to ordered form. It is entangled, like the mediæval mind itself, in a web of idle thoughts of which man as he is has ceased to be the centre.

When, in the Renaissance, that centre was recovered, and humanism became once more a conscious principle of thought, Roman design in architecture came with it as of right. But there was now a difference in its intent. Humanism has two enemies—chaos and inhuman order. In antiquity humanism strove principally against the primitive confusion of the world: its emphasis was laid on order: it clung to discipline and rule. Hence Greek architecture is the strictest of all styles of building, and Rome, in whatever outposts of Spain or Britain her legions were remotely quartered, there set a tiny Forum, and preserved without concession the imperial order of its plan. But in the thought of the Renaissance humanism was pitted, not against chaos, but against the inhuman rigour of a dead scholastic scheme, whose fault was not lack of logic, but excess of logic with a lack of relevance to man. Thus the emphasis of Renaissance humanism, in all its forms, was less on order than on liberty. And, in architecture, while it rebelled against the mere constructive logic of the Gothic style, while it returned with passion to the æsthetic logic of antiquity, it makes that logic serve the keen variety of life. It is no longer content to rest for ever in the restraint of classic equipoise and calm. It has learned the speech of architecture from Greece and Rome, but the Renaissance itself will choose what things that speech will say. Every value, every avenue of promise, it will explore, enjoy, express. Hence the insatiate curiosity, the haste, the short duration of its styles; hence the conversion of classic forms to the gay uses of baroque and rococo invention; hence the pliancy and swift recoveries of taste, of which our first chapter took account. But not the less does the Renaissance employ the language of Humanism; and hence its unsevered ties with classic architecture, its reliance on the 'Orders,' its perpetual study of the past. Still, as in antiquity, it speaks by mass, space, line, coherence; as in antiquity, it still builds through these a congruous setting to our life. It makes them echo to the body's music—its force and movement and repose. And the mind that is responsive to that harmony, it leads enchantingly among the measures of a dance in stone.

Virgil attends on Dante, and St. John, in the solitude of the Adriatic shrine he shares with Venus,[1] may ponder if ascetic energy is not best mated with a classical repose. The architecture of humanism has on its side the old world and the new; it has this repose and this energy. The spirit of perpetual change awoke in Europe, and architecture through four centuries gave to each change some shape of pagan beauty. A beauty of paganism, not its echo: Renaissance architecture is misconstrued wholly when we dismiss it as an imitative art. It served antiquity, not with the abject duty of a slave, nor always even with a scholar's patience, but masterfully, like a lover, with a like kindling of its proper powers. Brunelleschi, Bramante, Michael Angelo, Bernini had, as few can have it, their originality. But they followed on the past. The soil they built in was heavy with the crumbling of its ruins.

Yet every art that finds a penetrating pathway to the mind, and whose foundations are profoundly set, must needs have precedent and parallel, ancestors and heirs. For the penetrating paths are few; and, despite their baroque liberty of fancy, we can forget, as from the Palatine we watch the domes that overpeer the Forum, and see the front of San Lorenzo rise through the grey portico of Antoninus, how sheer an interval, with how vast a change of life, sunders two forms of art so congruous and familiar. Where classic power once stood, its shadow lingered: Mantegna, in the fifteenth century, painted men as Cæsars and made splendid with antique frieze and column the

[1] *San Giovanni in Venere*—the Baptist lodged with Venus— is a deserted church on the Abruzzi coast. The structure is Romanesque; the name more ancient still; but not until the Renaissance can its patrons have achieved their perfect reconciliation, which now the browsing goats do not disturb.

legends of the Church. The architects of humanism built deep. Like the heroes of Mantegna, they performed their labour in a Roman panoply, and in the broken temples of Rome dreamed their own vision, like his saints.

Epilogue 1924

I wrote these chapters ten years ago in a hope of which I was too young to realise the full temerity, conceiving that what I had to say might interest those who practise architecture, and also those who deal in philosophy; yet desiring also to conciliate those who require that a book, whatever else it may attempt, should not cease to be a book.

To carry my subject a stage further would be to enter a field where I could no longer entertain any such ambition. If I ever now attempt this, it will be in a separate and more technical form.

Since, however, the book as it stands has been fortunate enough to evoke some discussion, I would like here to say one or two things by way of epilogue and in reply.

It has been remarked with truth that the destructive portion of the book overweighs the constructive. But if the conclusions at which I arrive are rightly appreciated this will, I think, be seen to be inevitable.

My contention is that 'theory'—the attempt to decide architectural right and wrong on purely intellectual grounds—is precisely one of the roots of our mischief. Theory, I suppose, was what made the chatter on the scaffolding of the Tower of Babel. It is the substitute for tradition, and it has thriven and multiplied in England since our tradition terminated with Nash. I set out to show how untenable were the 'first principles' to which the teaching and the criticism of architecture usually make appeal. And I sought to indicate how these fallacies arose, and why they are still believed; for in these matters it is not enough to argue against an opinion: the opinion will remain unless the roots of it are exposed.

Moreover, since every error draws part of its vitality from

some measure of truth which is embedded in it, I sought in each case to lay bare that element of truth, and to show that these half-truths really derive, not from the theories they have been held to justify, but from that general principle of Humanism of which I speak in the eighth chapter.

To do this, however succinctly, was a long task. But the length of this portion is not of my choosing: it is determined by the number of the fallacies.

And if I have planted no full-blown theory on the ground thus cleared, this follows from the very nature of my contention. The most one can here do is to clear the ground: and then to indicate where the creative instinct lies, and in what it consists; and this I have attempted. But to seek to devise new codes for the operation of that instinct would be once more to intellectualise a faculty which is not in my opinion primarily an intellectual one at all.

If therefore an architect should reply: 'The first part of my problem is one of means and ends—mechanical means to a practical end—and is purely one of reasoning; but the further problem is one of taste, and here I can see for myself, and no mere argument can upset my felt preferences': if he says this I have little to object. Such an attitude was precisely that of the great architects of the past. Only there is this difference: that they were really saturated in their manner of building, and had not been schooled in the fallacies, while our modern teaching is haunted by the ghosts of all these errors, and in default of a live and veritable tradition we are expected to form an encyclopædic, and therefore necessarily superficial familiarity with 'styles.'

What we feel as 'beauty' in architecture is not a matter for logical demonstration. It is experienced, consciously, as a direct and simple intuition, which has its ground in that subconscious region where our physical memories are stored, and depends partly on these, and partly on the greater ease imparted to certain visual and motor impulses.

But, just as this process goes on (in most cases) below the field of consciousness, and rises to consciousness simply as 'pleasure,' so the training of the creative faculty will not lie so much in the analysis of that process, but rather in rendering it more sensitive. And we can only do this by *habituation* to such works as actually embody the values of Mass, Space, Line and Coherence—the 'humanised' values spoken of in Chapter Eight.

But if so, it matters greatly what our eyes habitually see, apart from our moments of concentrated research. Here, again, our masters had the advantage over us. They lived and moved among buildings where the values of Mass, Space and Line were often coherently displayed: their eyes were habituated to architecture of a relatively uniform intent. Our eyes, even if we know clearly what serious architecture is, have to search for it questioningly in a welter of commercial and municipal monstrosities. It is as though one had to tune a violin in the midst of a railway accident.

Meanwhile the heritage of humanist architecture on which we must depend for any education of architectural sensitiveness is being allowed to disappear. Our ecclesiastical authorities have awakened to the discovery that there are still some Wren churches which may, at a financial profit, be pulled down; and our Government, which lavishes money on futile academies and finds doles for the maintenance of museums and other cemeteries, is proceeding merrily to reimburse itself by the destruction of Regent Street; the only point of hope lying in the fact that the indignation aroused by this latter undertaking is at any rate markedly greater than when Mr. Norman Shaw's tumid edifice in the Quadrant first revealed how far we had outgrown the humanism of Nash.

Where then, practically speaking, are we led? Simply to the necessity of a more habitual, a more saturated familiarity with the tradition of humanist architecture. There is nothing novel, certainly, in this conclusion. But we shall perhaps have added this: that the tradition no longer will seem to hang on mere prestige and authority, but will be reinforced by a coherent view of the nature of architectural æsthetics. More than this, we shall look at the tradition itself from a slightly different angle. We shall no longer be concerned to square the works of Wren or Vanbrugh or Nash with our nineteenth-century code of fallacies, and they will appear in rather a different light.

Perhaps this is already happening. I noticed in the literature that appeared on the occasion of the recent Wren Bicentenary, that a number of writers were at pains to present Wren in the character of a great baroque architect. This is, I think, the 'new angle': it implies a better understanding both of the nature of baroque, and of the true inspiration of Wren. It is to attend to Wren's language where previous critics had looked at his parts of speech.

Here I would like to add a word on the subject of baroque. I find this book frequently referred to as though its main purpose were the defence of that style. But that is to take the part for the whole, and to confuse my thesis with my illustration. The baroque is in the highest degree interesting, because of its purely psychological approach to the problem of design, its freedom from mechanical and academic 'taboos,' for its use of scale, its search for Movement, its preoccupation with Mass composition and Spatial values. The mastery of these elements shown by the great baroque architects from Vignola to Bernini entitles the style they evolved to a very different estimate from that which was accorded to it by English writers. But my argument goes essentially beyond that particular question, and if I have come back so frequently to the subject of baroque, it is because it furnished a kind of acid test to the views I was considering. Further, if I defend the 'theatricality' of certain baroque buildings, it is in order to prove that there is no *a priori* architectural law to preclude such devices as they displayed. But 'theatricality' may be in place in one setting and out of place in another: on this point the enthusiasm of some writers who generously declare themselves my disciples has occasionally outrun my own. In any case, too much, it appears to me, has been made of the theatricality of baroque. If rather more attention had been paid to Roman palaces and rather less to Neapolitan churches, the essential gravity of the style would not have been so widely overlooked. There is a considerable affinity between baroque architecture and seventeenth century prose: the conceits, the flourishes, of Donne, for example, may or may not be to our taste,—it is an open question; but if they cause us to overlook the underlying rhythms, the spacious period and the weight, we have missed the very essentials of prose. Some critics of baroque lack, it may be, an ear for architecture.

While the contentions of my earlier chapters seem to have met with fairly wide assent—at any rate among the younger generation of architects, the view of architectural design which I have outlined in the eighth chapter has, I think, been sometimes misinterpreted. Thus I do not for a moment contend, as one writer has asserted, that physical memory supplies '*the whole* explanation of the nature and appeal of architecture.' Still less do I suggest that, in practice, 'an architect when faced with the problem of designing a house . . . proceeds to imagine physical states, and to take them as his theme.' It is obvious that in the sequence of considerations which confront an architect there are a hundred questions of fitness and common sense, which supply the first block and shape of his problem and compose nine-tenths of his difficulties, and there is an undoubted satisfaction in seeing these difficulties lucidly and reasonably resolved. But I have sought to prove that there is in architecture the possibility of a beauty which lies beyond this and cannot be reduced to these terms. Sooner or later the architect, in considering his alternative solutions, falls back quite simply upon an æsthetic preference. In attempting to show on what that perference is psychologically founded, I am not suggesting (1) that it forms the starting point of his problem, nor (2) that in practice he must necessarily be conscious of the psychological process which determines his choice. Most often he will experience it as a purely intuitive judgment of beauty into the sources of which he need not explore. Nevertheless I believe it useful to explore them, because the more conscious these processes become the more clearly will our creative effort be guided, and the less likely shall we be, at each juncture of hesitation, to be misled by some false theory into accepting a solution on quite irrelevant grounds.

If my critics have sometimes seemed to have overlooked essential passages, this, I recognise, is the natural penalty I pay for a condensed argument. Yet I was unwilling to expand it, thinking the wood might not be seen for the trees. The argument is close; but the book is short. And I myself would prefer, if need be, to read some things twice than to have read everything twice repeated.

The other day I was looking through the report of a discussion on this volume at the Royal Institute of British Architects. Among several too generous speakers was one, of whom I cannot think without gratitude and remorse. 'I have read (he averred) Mr. Scott's book fourteen times; and it is rather a tiresome book.'

Fourteen is too much. But to those who have kindly urged me to add a second volume, while at the same time raising objections which are explicitly answered in the first, I can only offer the example of my patient friend.

VILLA MEDICI,
FLORENCE, *March* 9, 1924.

FOUR

The Mechanical Fallacy

EIGHT

Humanist Values

NINE

Conclusion

Instruct and Delight

—+— —+—

Ken Anderson, Hitler and the Occult
Dusty Sklar, The Nazis and the Occult